90 ✓

DISCARD

i

Birth Power

Birth Power

The Case for Surrogacy

CARMEL SHALEV

Yale University Press *New Haven & London*

Designed by Richard Hendel
and set in Times Roman type
by Graphic Composition, Inc., Athens, Georgia.
Printed in the United States of America.

Library of Congress Cataloging-in-Publication Data
Shalev, Carmel.
   Birth power.

   Includes bibliographies and index.
      1. Surrogate mothers—Legal status, laws, etc.—United
States. 2. Parent and child (Law)—United States.
3. Surrogate mothers—Legal status, laws, etc. 4. Parent
and child (Law) I. Title [DNLM: 1. Mothers.   2. Parent-
Child Relations.   3. Reproduction.   4. Women's Rights.
WS105.5.F2   S528b]
KF540. S53 1989   346.7301'7   89-9114
ISBN 0-300-04216-7 (alk. Paper) 347.30617

The paper in this book meets the guidelines for
permanence and durability of the Committee on
Production Guidelines for Book Longevity of the
Council on Library Resources.

10 9 8 7 6 5 4 3 2 1

To Tal, and the women

of her generation

CONTENTS

ACKNOWLEDGMENTS

Many people contributed to the birth of this book. Several of them gave me indispensable support at moments when it was most needed. Special thanks to Jon Dalberg, Terri Clyde, Ala Elczewska, Jack Getman, Nancy Lewis, Joyce Lowry, Yvonne Masakowski, Ursula Pollak, Celina Romany, and Ann Scales. And to my father, Peter Elman, and my editor at Yale University Press, Marian Neal Ash.

This work was submitted in partial fulfillment of the requirements for a graduate degree in law at Yale Law School.

Birth Power

CHAPTER 1

Introduction

In these delicate vessels is borne onward through the ages
the treasure of human affection.
—*George Eliot*, Daniel Deronda

"We," they say, "have facts!" But facts aren't everything;
at least half the case consists in what you do with the
facts!
—*Fyodor Dostoyevski*, Crime and Punishment

The Case of Baby M

On March 27, 1986, a baby girl was born. Her mother named her
Sara Elizabeth, her father named her Melissa, and a trial judge in
Hackensack, New Jersey, later named her Baby M.[1] Approximately
one year before the baby's birth, Mary Beth Whitehead, a married
mother of two in her late twenties, had signed a surrogate mother
agreement with William Stern, a married, childless man going on
forty. Stern's parents were the sole members of his family to survive
the Holocaust, and he was the last in his bloodline. Unfortunately,
his wife suffered from symptoms of a disease that could be exacer-
bated by pregnancy, and she was unwilling to accept the physical
risks of carrying and bearing a child. Mary Beth Whitehead agreed
to attempt to conceive by artificial insemination with William Stern's
sperm, to carry the fetus to term, and after birth to surrender the
baby to Mr. Stern and his wife while relinquishing all her parental
rights. She was to be paid ten thousand dollars and all medical (including dental) expenses. At the trial she testified that she had been
motivated by the hope of "giving the most loving gift of happiness
to an unfortunate couple." The surrogate fee was to provide for her

children's long-range educational needs. Her husband, who had undergone vasectomy as a family-planning measure after the birth of his second child, deferred to his wife's wish to be a surrogate mother after initially opposing the idea.

The couples were introduced through an agency that had conducted a preliminary psychological evaluation of Mrs. Whitehead. According to the examiner's report, she expected to have strong feelings about giving up the child at birth but was sincere in her plan. At her first meeting with the Sterns she made it clear that all she wanted was an annual picture and letter report of the child's progress. Throughout the ensuing pregnancy they remained in close contact. Meanwhile the Sterns prepared a nursery room in their home and executed new wills naming the unborn child as contingent beneficiary.

At the moment of birth, however, Mary Beth Whitehead realized that she could not give up the baby. In violation of the agreement, she named her husband as the father on the infant's birth certificate. Three days after giving birth she left the hospital and took the baby home, where the Sterns came to claim her. Mrs. Whitehead appeared to be depressed, and she expressed her difficulties with the relinquishment. The next day she arrived at the Sterns' home after requesting permission by phone and said she wanted to take the baby with her for a one-week visit. The Sterns acquiesced out of concern for her mental health. Two weeks later, the child still with her, she allowed the Sterns to visit and announced that she had decided to keep the baby.

The Sterns then applied to a court to enforce the surrogacy agreement and obtained an order directing Mrs. Whitehead to return the baby to them. She subsequently abducted the child and fled the state with her family. The Whiteheads' whereabouts remained unknown to the Sterns for almost three months, during which time they lived as fugitives, moving from one hotel to another and staying with friends and relatives. The infant received no pediatric care during this period. Once the Whiteheads were located, local law enforcement officials took the baby into the care of the state authorities pursuant to a court order and subsequently transferred physical custody of the child to the Sterns.

Over the course of the following months the legal proceedings were widely covered and sensationalized by the press, exposing the most intimate details of the protagonists' private lives. Finally, a few days after Baby M's first birthday, the court announced its decision in the custody dispute. The father and mother of the child, it said, had entered an agreement of their own free wills on clear terms as to the child's future before she was ever physically conceived. Although conception could not be compelled, once it occurred, the terms of the contract were legally enforceable (subject to the mother's right to an abortion). A state could not ban or refuse to enforce reproductive contracts because this would violate the constitutional protection of the childless couple's personal liberty to find means to establish a family. The surrogate mother also had a constitutionally protected right to choose voluntarily to perform her services under a contract. If a "surrogate father" sperm donor is legally allowed to sell his sperm, the court argued, the surrogate mother must also be allowed to offer her reproductive services, as a matter of equal protection under the law.

The court concluded that the surrogate mother agreement was a valid contract which Mary Beth Whitehead had breached by refusing to surrender the child to the Sterns and to terminate her parental rights. Money damages could not possibly compensate William Stern for his loss, and the court would order specific performance of the contract subject to considerations of the child's best interests. The testimony showed that the Whiteheads had a history of economic and domestic instability, that they attached little importance to education (Mrs. Whitehead had dropped out of high school at fifteen), that Mary Beth Whitehead, the dominant spouse, was manipulative, impulsive, exploitive, and untruthful, and that Mr. Whitehead was an alcoholic. The Sterns, on the other hand, had a stable home environment and a high regard for education (both had Ph.D.'s), and had shown sensitivity to the child's needs and an ability to cope rationally with a trying emotional crisis. In this case there was no doubt that the child's interests would be best served by being placed in her father's sole custody. In the absence of laws that contemplated the novelty of a surrogacy situation, the court finally invoked the equitable maxim of treating as done that which ought to have been done and terminated Mary Beth Whitehead's parental rights in the child.

In re Baby M was the first American case to decide the issue of the legal effect and enforceability of a surrogacy agreement, and it did so in a style of judicial activism. In accepting the idea of a person's autonomy to contract with respect to reproductive activity, the judge not only departed from traditional rules of law (which he claimed did not apply to such a novel situation) but also took a position at odds with a contemporary trend to outlaw surrogacy. In two other common law[2] jurisdictions—the state of Victoria in Australia, and England—commercial surrogacy arrangements had already been criminalized following the recommendations of governmental committees of inquiry into the ethical and legal implications of rapidly developing reproductive technology. Indeed, amid serious concern about doctors playing god with embryonic life, commercial surrogacy was the only activity that these committees saw fit to outlaw with criminal sanctions.

The terms of reference of the first of these two committees, the Waller Committee in Victoria, restricted its inquiry to the employment of surrogate mothers as part of an in vitro fertilization program—as, for example, where a married woman with a nonfunctioning womb employs a surrogate mother to carry the pregnancy of an embryo conceived from her egg and her husband's sperm. The committee did address the issue of surrogacy in general, however, and concluded that "surrogate mother arrangements where fees are paid are, in reality, agreements for the purchase of a child. . . . Where such agreements contemplate the adoption of the child by the infertile wife, they are probably criminal conspiracies to controvert the provisions of the Adoption of Children Act." Such arrangements, it continued, were completely unacceptable as part of an in vitro fertilization program in Victoria. Whatever terms were employed, the buying and selling of a baby seemed clearly to be at the core of the arrangement. This had been condemned for generations and ought not to be permitted to reappear. The committee also recommended that "altruistic volunteer" agreements not be allowed in view of the potential conflicts of custody, deformed babies, and "the deliberate manufacture of a child for others."[3] Subsequently, the legislature enacted a statute—The Infertility (Medical Procedures) Act, 1984—which criminalized any commercial activity in connection with surrogacy by any person, including the surrogate mother, and rendered void any such agreement, formal or informal and whether or not for payment or reward.

In the second of these jurisdictions, in England, legislation was enacted on the recommendation of the Warnock Committee to criminalize the creation or operation of profit or nonprofit agencies whose purposes include the recruitment of women for surrogate pregnancy or arranging for individuals or couples to use the services of a carrying mother, including professionals who knowingly assist in surrogate pregnancy.[4] This committee did not extend criminality to the surrogate mother herself, however, being "anxious to avoid children being born to mothers subject to the taint of criminality." Yet it recommended statutory provisions to make all surrogacy agreements illegal, and therefore unenforceable, contracts. Only two of the committee's sixteen members dissented, stating that surrogacy could be beneficial to childless couples as a last resort and suggesting that surrogacy be allowed when arranged by a licensed nonprofit agency on referral from a gynecologist. While agreeing that the operation of for profit agencies should be prevented, the dissenting members thought that payments to the surrogate mother should not be a barrier to the child being adopted by the commissioning couple.

The Warnock Committee discussed surrogacy comprehensively, and its observations reflect mainstream thinking on the subject. Its grounds for outlawing surrogacy were of two distinct kinds: considerations pertaining to its perception of the proper social relations of reproduction, and considerations pertaining to the commercial aspect of such an arrangement.

With respect to the social relations of reproduction, the committee observed that

- the introduction of a third party into the process of procreation was an attack on the value of the marital relationship;
- surrogacy distorted the mother-child relationship, for the

woman deliberately allows herself to become pregnant with the intention to give up the child, "which is the wrong way to approach pregnancy";
- the separation of the child from the carrying mother, with whom it has strong bonds, is potentially damaging; and, finally,
- a woman should not be forced by legal sanctions to part with a child to which she has recently given birth.[5]

As for the commercial element,

- it was inconsistent with human dignity that a woman should use her uterus for financial profit and treat it as an incubator for someone else's child;
- it was degrading to the child, which, for all practical purposes, would have been bought for money;
- a woman ought not be asked to undertake the risks of pregnancy for another in order to earn money, and she should be protected against exploitation as a means to others' ends.[6]

Months after the *Baby M* case was first tried, the New Jersey Supreme Court reversed the decision on appeal as a matter of similar principle.[7] Though it upheld the lower court's decision to vest custody in Mr. Stern on grounds of the child's best interests, the court invalidated the surrogacy contract because it conflicted with state law and public policy (finding the payment of money to a surrogate mother "illegal, perhaps criminal, and potentially degrading to women"), reinstated Mary Beth Whitehead's rights as a (noncustodial) mother, and remanded the case to the trial court for a determination on visitation.

The surrogacy contract, stated the appeal court, conflicted with three statutory arrangements: (1) laws prohibiting the use of money in connection with adoptions; (2) laws requiring proof of parental unfitness or abandonment before termination of parental rights; and (3) laws making consent to adoption revocable and allowing surrender of the child only after birth. As for public policy, the whole purpose of the contract was to give the father the exclusive right to the child by destroying the rights of the mother, and this was at odds with both the settled principle that the child's best interests shall determine custody and the policy that the rights of natural parents are equal concerning their child. Finally, this contract was really for the sale of a child and in conflict with the public policy that prompted the prohibition of the payment of money in connection with adoption. Although in adoption the pregnancy is unwanted, whereas in surrogacy the mother's situation is intended, the essential evil is the same—taking advantage of a woman's circumstances in order to take away her child. Indeed, in the court's view, the surrogate mother "never makes a totally voluntary, informed decision, for quite clearly any decision prior to the baby's birth is, in the most important sense, uninformed, and any decision after that, compelled by a pre-existing contractual commitment, the threat of a lawsuit, and the inducement of a $10,000 payment is less than totally voluntary."[8] The fact that Mrs. Whitehead had actually *agreed* to the surrogacy arrangement was irrelevant, since "there are, in a civilized society, some things that money cannot buy."[9]

The court also ruled on constitutional issues. First, the rights of procreation, privacy, and self-determination asserted by the Sterns did not imply that the father had a fundamental right to custody of the child when opposed by the claim of the mother. And their right to procreate by methods of their own choice was limited by the state's interest in protecting the innocent child. The Sterns also raised an equal protection argument in reference to the state statute granting a husband parental rights to a child conceived by his wife, with his consent, through artificial insemination with sperm from a donor. They contended that Mrs. Stern was in precisely the same position as the husband in the artificial insemination statute: being infertile, her spouse begets a child by arrangement with a third party on the understanding that the couple will raise the child. The court dismissed this argument, finding a sufficient basis for the state to distinguish the two situations in the difference between the time it takes to provide sperm for artificial insemination and the time invested in a nine-month pregnancy.

The court concluded that, although present law did not permit the surrogacy arrangement in the case at bar, there was no prohibition against surrogacy if the surrogate mother volunteered, without any payment, and retained the right to change her mind and to assert her parental rights. It also suggested that there might be room for legislative consideration of surrogacy, as an opportunity to focus on the overall implications of the new reproductive biotechnology—in vitro fertilization, preservation of sperm and eggs, embryo implantation, and the like.

Similar controversy had surrounded artificial insemination, the oldest and most widespread medical reproductive technique, when it first appeared in legal context in the 1950s and 1960s. Adultery and illegitimacy were key terms in the adjudication of the first cases but were problematic as norms of conduct for reproduction without sex. At the same time, the laws of adoption seemed inappropriate to a situation in which the mother and child were biologically related and no one needed to know that the woman's husband was not the child's father. Eventually, the courts developed a scheme (later adopted by the legislatures) that distinguished between the biological father and the legal father, divesting the anonymous sperm donor of all parental rights and responsibilities and vesting them in the husband who consents to his wife's artificial insemination with donated sperm.

If disputes arise out of surrogacy relations, the courts may apply the law according to any one of these three existing models: adultery-illegitimacy, adoption, or donor artificial insemination. In a general sense, the *Baby M* trial court adopted the artificial insemination model (giving legal effect to the initial intentions of the persons who entered into the surrogacy agreement), whereas the appeal court applied the adoption model (finding the arrangement illegal). Issues of adultery or illegitimacy have limited legal significance nowadays and did not appear particularly relevant to the case. However, these two legal concepts, together with the institution of marriage, once constituted the traditional common law of reproductive relations; that is, they determined the scope of permitted sexual activity and at least on the face of it defined the parent-child relation as a matter of biology. To the extent that surrogacy raises issues about the scope of permitted reproductive collaboration and about party autonomy in defining a nonbiological parent-child relation, these traditional norms must highlight any theoretical discussion of the contemporary law of reproduction. The first half of this work examines these three models for regulating reproductive relations and defining parent-child relations as background for the analysis of surrogacy that follows in the second half, which considers the issue of defining parent-child relations in surrogate mother arrangements in terms of contracts for personal services.

A Feminist Approach

Even though the *Baby M* appellate court ordered that the child remain in her father's custody, feminists who had rallied to support Mary Beth Whitehead throughout the lengthy legal proceedings applauded its principled decision. They felt that the woman who spends nine months in intense emotional interaction with a fetus has a right to change her mind and to say whether she wants the child. "Are contracts sacred?" asked Phyliss Chesler. "Are they more sacred than the bond between a mother and child? What makes a contract more important than contraction? A legal conception more honorable than a biological one? Is legalism's 'pound of flesh' more worthy of a human being than 'the quality of mercy'?"[10] The court, she claimed, had employed feminist language and concepts, showing sensitivity to the ideal of gender neutrality and to the reality of gender differences. Although men and women are to be treated equally, "surrogate uteruses" and sperm donors are not identical. The decision meant that the court had recognized a natural bond between a birth mother and her infant that does not exist between a father and his infant.

The thesis that I propose also stems from a feminist philosophy but reaches the converse conclusion. Biology is clearly a double-edged sword. During my initial research, I discovered that much of the ethical writing on the new reproductive technologies was concerned with the sanctity of fetal life and the marital relation. Yet amid the serious debate on the morality of medical reproduction, only surrogacy has been addressed in terms of criminal norms. It occurred to me that the reason for this was the untraditional role that women play in these arrangements. The idea of paying women for deliberate reproductive activity does, indeed, strain our moral sensibilities, if only because we find it hard to distinguish between the sale of a baby and the sale of female reproductive services.

Technically, the key question is whether the law will recognize a surrogacy agreement as a contract that may be enforced against a rescinding surrogate. Does it matter whether the surrogate's change of mind occurs before or after birth? Whether she was promised payment or volunteered to do the job for free? Whether she is carrying a fetus that was conceived in her womb from her own egg or one that was implanted in her womb after laboratory fertilization from another woman's egg?

These legalisms raise weighty considerations of social policy. Is the law to countenance an arrangement that is tantamount to the sale of a baby? Does not a woman have an inalienable "natural" right to the fruit of her womb? Even if we distinguish between the sale of a baby and the sale of reproductive services, will such arrangements not create a caste of breeder women, as ripe for economic exploitation as the common prostitute? Ought not the law protect women and restrain the market and its modus operandi, the contract, from encroaching on one of the last remaining bastions of humanist values, the realm of family relations? If so, is criminalization of surrogacy the answer? Given the present dimensions of infertility and the unsatisfied demand for adoptable children, would that not merely expose women to exploitation and victimization with no form of legal protection?

I chose to address all these questions within the context of an even broader issue: the legal definition of parent-child relations. Until fairly recently, parenthood seemed to be a matter of biological predetermination. Reproductive medicine, however, differentiates biological and social roles of parenthood; the sperm donor is not considered the legal father of the artificial insemination child. Moreover, the more sophisticated technique of in vitro fertilization allows the possibility of separating biological roles of genetic and gestational motherhood. How will the law then define legal motherhood?

A closer look at the legal tradition that equated biological with legal parenthood shows that the "natural" family was also regulated by the legal norms of marriage, adultery, and illegitimacy. These combined to form what I call the blood institution, a social construct that employed a double standard of sexual-reproductive conduct, resting on patriarchal notions of biological gender and female inferiority. Marriage functioned, among other things, to transcend the uncertainty of biological paternity through control of women's behavior. The norms of adultery and illegitimacy were essentially punitive measures against women who were sexually active outside marriage.

The legal development of the nonbiological family of adoption retained some of the punitive nature of this scheme. The model of closed, secret adoption severs all connection between biological and adoptive families. In so doing it mandates the legal death of the birth mother while affording the child legal rebirth in the adoptive family. Nevertheless, if we consider adoption together with the subsequent innovation of artificial insemination, we find a trend from status (biological predetermination) to contract in the constitution of the legal family. In other words, individual autonomy in determining the consequences of reproductive activity, rather than biological connection, becomes a fundamental principle of the legal definition of parenthood. This trend stops, however, at surrogacy, where we find a conflicting tendency to outlaw the activity. How do we explain this tension?

One possible answer is that we have reached the limits of irreducible biological difference that must be accommodated within a vision of gender equality. Another answer—which I propose—is that this is one more facet of the double standard of sexual-reproductive morality. It seems to me that the refusal to acknowledge the legal validity of surrogacy agreements implies that women are not competent, by virtue of their biological sex, to act as rational, moral agents regarding their reproductive activity. An alternative scheme, I suggest, might recognize the constitutional privacy of individuals, regardless of gender, to define legal parenthood as a matter of autonomous decision-making authority, before conception. So long as the normative consequences of the reproductive collaboration are clarified before the potential human life begins, the interests of the child-to-be and the integrity of the legal family can be adequately protected. Responsibility, not right, is a key concept in this scheme, and conception is the moment at which it must be exercized.

What is more, the economic reality of human relations is such (perhaps unfortunately so) that money is the binding factor of agreements. A volunteer is no more than a volunteer. Therefore, I ultimately advocate the legitimation of the monetary element in surrogate mother arrangements, through recognition of them as legally binding reproductive contracts. This view not only entails a role for reason in the conception of human life but also strikes at the core of a series of ideological dichotomies that are fed by the idea of biological gender difference: public-private, market-family, and production-reproduction. My argument is that a concept of wages for reproduction can transform reproductive consciousness in a manner that transcends male-female biological difference to an androgynous mode of human being, while allowing women to reclaim the procreative power that has been subsumed under patriarchy as a mark of their inferiority.

From Status to Contract

All cultures and societies have attempted to control reproduction through the prevention and promotion of human fertility.[11] Present practices are distinguished from these precedents by the body of knowledge that informs them, that is, the modern science of biomedicine. Maternal-child health programs, Dr. Spock pediatrics, neonatal intensive care, hospitalized childbirth and cesarian-section deliveries, prenatal maternal care and diagnosis of fetal abnormalities, noncoital (that is, without coitus, or sexual intercourse) methods of conception, surgical abortion and sterilization, and prescription contraceptives are all indications of a process that can be termed the medicalization of reproduction. This process is characterized by the scientific objectification of reproductive activity and by the usurpation of women's control over their own bodies by a male-dominated medical profession.

The potential of laboratory fertilization, genetic manipulation, and gestation in an artificial womb gave rise to Aldous Huxley's classic vision in *Brave New World* of a dehumanized conveyor-belt system of human reproduction, initiated by detached political actors, to achieve a rigidly stratified totalitarian polity of individuals programed for predetermined social functions. The realization of this vision is obviously not inevitable.[12] Science supplies means—mere instruments—to attain ends conceived by individual and institutional decision makers. The understanding of causal relations allows us to fashion tools (technology) to intervene in natural processes and control them to serve human purposes. But the dynamics of technological development are informed at every moment ad infinitum by human choice, and scientific knowledge in and of itself provides no clues as to the ways in which such choice is to be exercised.

Medicalized reproduction indeed affords many new choices, particularly in the field of infertility therapy. At the same time the authority to make decisions about those choices has been largely assumed by medical professionals, who claim scientific objectivity. In fact, though, science as a human endeavor is inherently imperfect, since it rests on observation and comprehension of an environment that is infinitely affected by human activity. When human reproduction is the object of inquiry, the nature of the observed process compounds the innate subjectivity of the scientist. Human reproduction is not merely an objective, natural process occurring in an external reality; it is also—perhaps primarily—an arena of social interaction.

Feminist method, as Ann Scales points out, is precisely a critique of objectivity and the aspiration to abstract things from their social context.[13] This critique is particularly important when dealing with the area of human reproduction, in which objective biological differences have been taken to excuse women's inferior position in society. From the scientific standpoint human reproduction is a natural biological process of a mammalian species in which the female, like her animal counterpart, plays a central role. Patriarchy embraces this idea, taking the male experience of existence as the point of reference to distinguish humanity from other forms of animal life and defining the female in relation thereto as an Other, destined by her reproductive biology to exist somewhere in limbo between the animal and the human. As Simone de Beauvoir put it, woman's reproductive capacity is regarded as a natural, passive function by which the species repeats itself biologically, whereas man transcends his animal nature by conceiving of projects that subject nature to his control.

> On the biological level a species is maintained only by creating itself anew; but this creation results only in repeating the same Life in more individuals. But man assures the repetition of Life while transcending Life through Existence; by this transcendence he creates values that deprive pure repetition of all value. In the animal, the freedom and variety of male activities are vain because no project is involved. . . . Whereas in serving the species, the human male also remodels the face of the earth, he creates new instruments, he invents, he shapes the future. In setting himself up as sovereign, he is supported by the complicity of woman herself. For she, too, is an existent, she feels the urge to surpass, and her project is not mere repetition but transcendence toward a different future. . . . Her misfortune is to have been biologically destined for the repetition of Life.[14]

The notion of woman's reproductive destiny and passivity still colors discourse on human reproduction. Female reproductive functioning is supposed to be prerational, not subject to the rule of reason. And the active personality of the reproducing female is relegated to relative obscurity while attention focuses on the formation of the person-to-be in her body, framing ethical discussion of the new technology mainly in terms of the value of prenatal life.

From a feminist standpoint (not exclusive to persons born female) human reproduction is qualitatively distinct in its "human" essence, which is "conscious," "moral," and "political," interweaving the existent persons (male and female) in a social context of relation and interaction. In this vein Mary O'Brien focuses on the social relations of human reproduction and identifies two "historical moments" in the transformation of reproductive consciousness. The first was the discovery of biological paternity, the abstract conceptualization of a cause-and-effect relationship between copulation and childbirth, which triggered a fundamental transformation in male reproductive consciousness. The second was the discovery of contraception, the realization of choice and control in the process of becoming a parent, which triggered an equally significant transformation in female reproductive consciousness.[15]

Indeed, the male experience of reproduction is tainted fundamentally by the uncertainty of paternity. For the male lacks a tangible experiential link between generations, whereas the connection between female and child finds physical expression in pregnancy and the labor of giving birth. As O'Brien writes:

At the primordial level of genetic continuity, of the continuity of the species, men are separated from natural continuity. Male reproductive consciousness is a consciousness of discontinuity. Underlying the doctrine that man makes history is the undiscussed reality of why he must. The alienation of his seed separates him from natural genetic continuity, which he therefore knows only as an idea. To give this idea substance, man needs praxis, a way of unifying what he knows as real with actual worldly reality. Men must therefore make, and have made, artificial modes of continuity.[16]

The male transcends the inherent uncertainty of his biological continuity by asserting normative control over women's sexual behavior. Hence the blood institution as the artificial mode of continuity that defines the social relations of reproduction and the essence of the gender structure of patriarchal society.

The technology of noncoital conception appears to have the potential to transform both male and female reproductive consciousness. First, the availability of alternatives to sexual reproduction introduces new elements of choice. Whereas contraception makes it possible to choose whether to reproduce, the new reproductive technology makes it possible to choose *how* to reproduce. Second, whereas contraception allows for sex without reproduction, noncoital conception allows for reproduction without sex. Third, noncoital conception affords a hitherto unknown degree of control over the initiation of the reproductive process and its timing. John A. Robertson sums this up by distinguishing between negative reproductive freedom (the right not to reproduce) and positive reproductive freedom—the right to reproduce "when, with whom and by what means one chooses."[17] Finally, all of the above applies regardless of biological gender.

The control of conception is evident in the technique of in vitro fertilization, in which ovulation is monitored and controlled hormonally and mature eggs are identified by observation before their natural release from the follicles, obtained by surgical procedure or suction, and, finally, fertilized with sperm in a petri dish. In the natural course of affairs, ovulation and conception are intangible and involuntary, and this technical possibility of both planning and observing conception provides a concrete basis for the potential transformation of reproductive consciousness.

At the same time the technology alters the social relations of reproduction significantly. The involvement of medical professionals removes the activity of conception from the sphere of private sexual relations in the marital bed to the public space of the hospital, raising the general issue of expanding medical control over matters of life and death. And beyond the dissociation of reproduction from sex, the technology breaks down the role of parent into distinct genetic, gestational, and social functions: it is technically possible to fertilize an egg from Woman A with sperm from Man B, to implant the fertilized egg for gestation in the womb of Woman C, and to place the child in the custody of a couple—Man D and Woman E—for rearing. In other words, the technology entails a collaborative project of various actors that departs from the traditional norm of sexual reproduction within a marital relation and might result in a social parent-child relation that is based on no biological connection whatsoever.

Given the range of options, the question is: If choices are to be made, who is to make them? This is a matter of allocating decision-making authority for technical control over initiating the human reproductive process, and for employing noncoital means of conception to the end of establishing a parent-child relation. In terms of social policy the question leads to a normative evaluation of the roles of the individual, the family, the medical profession, and the state in controlling reproductive activity.

Since the purpose of collaborative reproduction is to bring a new person into being, the principles that govern social relations of reproducing adults must clarify the legal responsibility for the consequences of choice—that is, for the social parenting of the resulting child. Whereas the traditional law of reproduction in principle equated legal parenthood with biological parenthood, the noncoital technology calls for further examination of the rules that define a legal parent-child relation. This presents another issue of policy regarding the normative consequences of biological reproductive functions. Given the traditional perception of fundamental biological differences in gender, the question is whether a double standard should inform the regulation of collaborative reproductive activity.

Because of the social inequities women suffer under the double standard, my bias has been to invent a scheme that would be neutral in terms of gender. At the same time the overwhelming opposition to surrogacy in the literature seems to reinforce women's confinement in what de Beauvoir called the subjectivity of the womb and to perpetuate the stereotype of the fickle female who changes her mind, and it has incited me to question the many self-evident truths about women and childbearing that feed these attitudes. The idea of personal agency in contracting to become a parent seeks to empower women to reclaim the power of their wombs and to wield it responsibly with due respect for the biological vulnerability of men who must be able to trust and depend on women if they are to become fathers.

The blood institution was part of a hierarchical feudal social order that has given way to the modern postindustrial state. The nature of this transition, from a feudal society stratified rigidly according to the circumstances of a person's birth to a social order based on principles of equality and liberty, is captured in Sir Henry Maine's often quoted dictum that "the movement of the progressive societies has hitherto been a movement from status to contract."[18] The term *status* means in this context that a person's position in society, or legal relation to other persons, is determined by factors outside his or her control, such as family affiliation. (In contemporary law, *status* is still used to denote specific social relations, such as marriage or labor relations, which, once established, entail definite, mandatory legal consequences.) In modern society, however, a person may generally acquire social, economic, or political position as an independent agent by means of free agreement or contract with others. Feudal and modern society thus contrast in the manner by which social position is attained: where status formerly was "ascribed," now it is "achieved."[19]

In ancient society, according to Maine, a person had no identity in public life beyond that determined by family affiliation, and in the private realm of the kinship group the individual was subject to the uncontrolled authority of the patriarch. The movement from status to contract freed the individual from "domestic despotism" as much as it recognized the individual's independent public existence. The transition also indicated a sophistication in political organization. The notion of blood kinship is a symbol of primitive community relations, simultaneously binding the family within itself and separating it from other families. Ancient law was framed as a system of small, independent corporations, the families. Corporations, as artificial creatures of law, do not die, so that male bloodlines were perpetual and inextinguishable. The history of political ideas, Maine asserted, began with the assumption that kinship in blood was the sole possible ground of community organization, and the creation of the artificial family through the legal fiction of adoption was essential to the political expansion of society beyond the bounds of kinship.[20]

The transition from status-based relations to social arrangements organized mainly around contract also involves a shift from unquestioned traditional forms to rationally contrived ones[21] and is marked by the gradual dissolution of family dependency and the emergence of the self-determining individual. A movement from status to contract in defining parent-child relations would be a progressive step

acy figured prominently in the discussion. Facing new
which reproduction occurred outside marriage without
ourse, the courts were forced to examine the social pol-
ng the blood institution. The idea that control of female
a means to control female reproduction, rather than an
, found immediate expression.

t reported case in an English-speaking jurisdiction—the
ase of *Orford v. Orford* in 1921—the question arose
arried woman who allegedly conceived through artificial
n with donor sperm had committed adultery, thereby for-
right to alimony. Her counsel argued that sexual inter-
a necessary ingredient in adultery, resting in the "moral
of such conduct. The court disagreed. It considered the
adultery to lie in its effect on the marriage relation, the
ject of which was "the perpetuation of the human race":

ssence of the offense of adultery consists, not in the
rpitude of the act of sexual intercourse, but in the vol-
urrender to another person of the reproductive powers
ties of the guilty person; and any submission of those
to the service or enjoyment of any person other than the
l or the wife comes within the definition of 'adul-
. .

al intercourse is adulterous because in the case of a
it involves the possibility of introducing into the family
usband a false strain of blood. . . . That such a thing
be accomplished in any other than the natural manner
ly never entered the heads of those who considered the
n before.[1]

view, marriage was a kind of reciprocal contract between a
a woman by which they exchanged exclusive access to each
ody for the purpose of establishing a family.[2] The notion of
presupposes the existence of two equal, legal subjects as
o the marriage relation, but under the common law this
t have been the case, since until fairly recently a woman
idered to be the property of a man—either her father or her
—and not, therefore, a legal subject in her own right. This

toward freeing ourselves from the yoke of traditional gender relations and achieving a just, egalitarian society.

The nature of my discourse is essentially legal. Generally speaking, law is an institutionalized body of rules to govern social relations that includes mechanisms to adapt to changing conditions. Law
embodies a tension between tradition and progress and acts as a sta-
bilizing monitor of social change. At the same time, the law—
rooted in tradition—tends to lag behind social change.

The subject of this work is an area of human activity that has not
only undergone rapid technological development but also touches on
fundamental facets of male-female relations, which appear to be
concurrently redefining themselves in many other respects. Since the
law governing these novel relations of human reproduction is in the
initial stages of development, I have attempted to put forward a
strong critique of its traditional principles. I have also taken the liberty of suggesting an alternative normative framework for the regulation of reproductive relations. The work thus contains three interwoven analyses: descriptive, critical, and prescriptive.

The prescriptive component is informed in theory by some new
normative concepts but ultimately employs traditional legal discourse, extrapolating new rules from established legal principles
(constitutional privacy, for example) that are merely applied in a
novel context. The main concepts of reproductive agency and responsibility, with their focus on the moment of conception, set a
high standard of conduct in the social relations of reproduction. This
has made me pause to consider whether that standard might not be
unrealistic or unreasonable.

Numerous persons have suggested that the position I take is even
cruel, if one contemplates the concrete situation of a particular
woman who made a simple mistake within the economic and political constraints of a capitalist-patriarchal system. Perhaps, indeed,
there is a point where reason reaches its limit and must make way
for emotion. Nevertheless, the inquiry has merit if it merely enriches
the discourse by raising thorny perspectives to highlight the complexity of the issue.

Erich Fromm, discussing the norm of love—feeling responsible for and one with your neighbor, rather than respecting his or her rights as a distant and separate being—also addressed this difficulty. "If our whole social and economic organisation is based on each one seeking his own advantage," he asked, "if it is governed by the principle of egotism tempered only by the ethical principle of fairness, how can one do business, how can one act within the framework of existing society and at the same time practise love?" Acknowledging that the *principle* underlying capitalistic society and the *principle* of love (responsibility) are incompatible, he still hoped for the realization of the ideal. "Because the spirit of a production-centered, commodity-greedy society is such that only the non-conformist can defend himself successfully against it . . . important and radical changes in our social structure are necessary, if love is to become a social and not a highly individualistic, marginal phenomenon."[22]

The law generally labors under a tension between the ideal and the real. This tension is resolved through the discretion that judges exercise in the idiosyncratic application of any given norm, whereby human imperfection is accommodated. Every rule has its exceptions, none is absolute. The question is whether the rule of surrogacy should be that promises be kept and agreements enforced, with exceptions in justified cases, or that there be a right of rescission, with exceptions in justified cases. The idealistic tone that accompanies my argument in favor of the rule of enforceability is a consequence of a faith in the human potential to transform reproductive consciousness and make a better future for our daughters and sons.

CHAPTER 2

The Biologica

She remembered—betwixt a
of the neighboring townspeo
for the child's paternity, and
attributes, had given out tha
demon offspring; such as, ev
had occasionally been seen o
of their mother's sin, and to p
purpose.

—Nathaniel Hawthorne, The

Any discussion of the paren
logical family unit, which
form of social organization.
proper subject for the law. In
tional norms that embodies
forms the basis for any discu
relations. The building blocks
are the norms of marriage, ad
constitute what I call "the blo
constitution of the patriarchal
institution based on patrilineag
relationship to the father. They
are first defined by their reprod
that respect by behavioral con
such the blood institution is perv
dard of sexual and reproductive

Controlling Reproduction

When legal issues of reproductiv
to artificial insemination with dor

and illegitim
situations in
sexual interc
icy underlyi
sexuality is
end in itself

In the firs
Canadian c
whether a n
inseminatio
feiting her
course was
turpitude"
offense of
primary ob

The e
moral tu
untary s
or facul
powers
husband
tery'. . .

Sexu
woman
of the
would
probab
questic

In this
man and
other's b
contract
parties t
could no
was con
husband

fundamental inequality of the traditional marriage relation was firmly rooted in spousal reproductive relations. An adulterous act was one that threatened the marriage relation by raising the possibility of introducing spurious heirs into the husband's bloodline. This could only be a female offense, determined as such in order to overcome the intrinsic uncertainty of biological paternity.

In the Judeo-Christian tradition, the monogamous biological family's structural norms of marriage, adultery, and illegitimacy are seen as moral dictates from God. This is most evident in contemporary Catholic teachings on birth technology. In a doctrinal statement on human reproduction and biomedical intervention in 1987, the Vatican once more put forward "the divine law" as the basis of its position on the application of technology to human life and its beginnings. This supposed "natural" moral law derives from rational reflection on the true nature of the human being and postulates two fundamental criteria for the moral evaluation of reproductive techniques: the dignity of the life of the human being called into existence, and the special nature of the transmission of human life in marriage. From this perspective, marriage is "the bond existing between husband and wife [that] accords the spouses, in an objective and inalienable manner, the exclusive right to become father and mother solely through each other." The initiation of human life is morally licit only when it results from the sexual union of a man and woman in marriage "as the fruit of the conjugal act specific to the love between spouses." Man's moral duty is to realize his vocation from God to the gift of love and the gift of life. Given that individual human life, the family, and the institution of marriage are constitutive elements of civil society and its order, political authority is obliged to insure that the civil law is regulated according to these fundamental norms of divine law.[3] In consequence, this approach would deem surrogate childbearing unacceptable.

The Uncertainty of Paternity

The fundamental inequality of the sexes in marriage is not expressly apparent in the religious view of a static relation dictated by nature.

But it does become evident when one attempts a secular explanation of the blood institution. Friedrich Engels described the monogamous family in the light of Lewis H. Morgan's anthropological research as one stage in the active adaptation of a social organization to changing economic conditions. In primitive societies we find group marriage, which is the possession in common of husbands and wives within a broad but definite family circle. In all forms of group family, Engels continued, the father of a child is uncertain, but not the mother. Since descent can be proved only on the mother's side, the female line of descent alone is recognized. The transition to the patrilineal family necessarily entailed the overthrow of "mother right," a revolution that was "the world historical defeat of the female sex," coinciding with the victory of private property over communal property. The accumulation of wealth in the hands of the husband, who controlled the instruments of labor necessary to obtain food (including cattle and slaves) according to the division of labor within the family at the time, created an impulse to overthrow, in favor of his children, the traditional order of inheritance. The monogamous family emerged for the sole purpose of propagating children of undisputed paternity, which meant that it was imperative to insure the wife's fidelity. Hence the subjugation of the female sex to male supremacy.[4]

Women's relinquishment of mother right requires some kind of explanation. To the extent that economic wealth came under male control, women would have an interest in male inheritance so that their sons could inherit the wealth of their fathers. For under mother right a man's property passed on his death to his birth family (his blood relations on his mother's side) rather than to his wife or children by marriage. Also, given the superior physical strength of the male—and therefore the constant threat of rape or involuntary sexual surrender in group marriage—women could conceivably have realized an interest in limiting their sexual accessibility through marriage to one man only. Or perhaps it was simply that the combined power of the male's economic and physical supremacy forced the overthrow of mother right.

Simone de Beauvoir also suggests a connection between the emergence of private property and the situation of women in society, but she considers this to be only a partial explanation of a reality that combines economic and mystical factors. Woman's reproductive capacity embodies the magical fertility of nature, in the face of which man experiences fear and powerlessness. The principle of male descent satisfies man's existential need to master nature and the female who remains in bondage to its mysterious processes. In transferring material possessions to his own offspring, man assures his ancestral survival on earth and attains immortality.[5]

Whether there was ever a period of universal mother right in the actual history of human society—which appears to be a matter of pure speculation—the idea of a paternal bloodline clearly contradicts the biological reality of uncertain paternity. Indeed, the tension this produces has psychological ramifications. The individual male proves his manliness by producing a male heir, and failure to do so is his shame. Male infertility is thus a closely guarded secret, if not actually suppressed or denied by blaming it on the female. After all is said and done, the open question whether his children are really his haunts the male in the cuckold's fear. The anxiety about female infidelity feeds a basic mistrust of all women.

To maintain the pretense of certain paternity, the individual male must have the backing of the community of males. In primitive societies the vindication of his honor was a cause for concerted violence in the form of the "blood revenge." Later, social recognition of individual paternity claims was embodied in the property rights of the husband. In marriage he acquired exclusive control over a woman and her potential offspring, much as he had over cattle and slaves, and separated her physically from other men in the private space of the domestic home. The children of a married woman were presumed, as a matter of law, to be the children of her husband, while unauthorized female sexual activity was heavily penalized. A married woman's sexual relations with a man other than her husband were criminalized in the norm of adultery, and the offspring of a sexual relation outside marriage were generally branded as illegitimate.[6]

The Double Standard

Under the common law—a system that evolved in England around the thirteenth century—marriage became a transaction between a woman's father and her prospective husband to transfer ownership of the woman. As chattel, the woman could neither hold rights nor transfer them.[7] The husband was therefore the only member of the family to be recognized as a legal subject; his wife and minor children were mere objects within his private domain. In such a subject-object relation the subject has the prerogative to control the uses of the object and to define its social value. The modern principle of familial autonomy, expressing the law's hands-off attitude toward domestic affairs, has its origin in this concept of familial relations.

The patrilineal family thus entailed a double standard of sexual morality that enjoined monogamy on the female while allowing the male great sexual freedom. Strict marital fidelity was required of the wife, so as to avoid the risk of inheritance by some other man's child. Monogamy was accompanied by the professional prostitution of unmarried women, with whom the husband could continue to exercise sexual freedom. The contradiction of marriage and prostitution was concealed in the condemnation of the prostitute, who was despised, rejected, and cast to the fringes of society.[8]

The ideological scheme of patriarchy gave a woman one choice: she could be either a wife or a harlot. In marriage a woman's motherhood was revered and idolized; outside marriage it was abhorred and condemned. As a result women were divided, often along lines of class and race, into two classes—virtuous madonna (virgin) and fallen whore.[9] The married woman felt no sympathy for out-of-wedlock motherhood, for the illegitimate child's claim to her husband's inheritance could be made only at the expense of her own children's position within the legitimate family.[10] Under patriarchy men appropriated women but compensated for that forfeited freedom by the social position, shelter, and support that came with marriage. In a way, the wife depended for her "pedestalized" moral status on the degradation of the prostitute. Since a woman's social value derived from her capacity to continue the bloodline of her husband, the unmarried mother posed a threat to the very foundations of a woman's limited social respectability.

Church doctrine on marriage reinforced these values. Reproducing within marriage a woman would find the comfort of God's spiritual love. Reproducing outside marriage she would merely reaffirm Eve's original sin. Only through a legitimate relation to a man could a woman hope to attain some measure of spiritual existence. Although childbearing was a bodily function, in itself devoid of spiritual value, a woman could redeem herself by bringing forth children within a God-blessed union to raise them in accord with divine morality through her own impeccable personal example.[11]

Adultery

The double standard of sexual morality within the patrilineal family is evident in the discriminatory application of the legal norm of adultery. In Jewish law, for example, the duty "to be fruitful and multiply" was the husband's religious obligation and not the wife's, one reason being that the man was regarded as active and the woman as passive in sexual relations. In spite of her passive sexual nature, however, a woman was held criminally liable for the pleasure she derived from sexual offenses committed upon her with her consent. A married woman's infidelity was and remains a bar to the continuation of a marriage. An adulterous wife is "forbidden" to her husband as well as to her lover—divorce from her husband is compulsory and marriage to her lover is prohibited. Yet the husband's extramarital sexual activity is not in itself grounds for divorce.[12]

Ecclesiastical jurisdiction over marriage was firmly established in England by the mid-twelfth century. Before this, a husband who caught his wife in the act of adultery could with impunity kill either or both of the guilty parties. The ecclesiastical courts introduced the milder punishment of whipping and other "bodily penances." A man could divorce an adulterous wife and remarry when he chose to. The wife forfeited her right to dower and was allowed to remarry only after five years.[13] In nineteenth-century Britain the civil courts gained jurisdiction over family affairs. The Custody of Infants Law of 1839, which recognized the mother's right to custody of her children, was the first statute to encroach on the common law rule of the father's absolute custody. A mother who had been judged guilty of adultery, however, was not entitled to custody of her children. A father might be deprived of custody on grounds of exceptionally culpable behavior, but adultery did not fall within that category. In other words, adulterous conduct reflected on the mother's fitness to parent a child but not on the father's. Likewise, the Matrimonial Causes Act of 1857, which introduced judicial divorce in England, applied a double standard of adultery. The husband could succeed in a divorce action on the sole ground of his wife's adultery, whereas the wife was required to establish an additional matrimonial offense, such as cruelty or desertion.[14]

The norm of adultery in the United States in the nineteenth century varied from state to state. In some jurisdictions adultery served as a ground for divorce only in cases of the wife's sexual misconduct, as evidenced by criminal statutes that defined adultery plainly as intercourse between a man and a married woman. In other states, divorce statutes required a wife to prove that her husband "lived in adultery," whereas he needed to prove only a single act of adultery on her part. When divorce was granted on grounds of the wife's adultery, she was invariably declared morally unfit to have custody of her child. In some states a child could be adopted without the mother's consent if she had acted in "open and notorious adultery." Today this legal measure is usually justified only in extreme cases of neglect, desertion, cruelty, alcoholism, or drug addiction.[15]

In this manner a woman's deviation from the norm of marital sex bore concrete consequences that were enforced by the state, through its legislative and judicial branches, as a matter of public concern. A woman's very social status as wife or mother hinged on her sexual propriety. To strip her of these was to make her an outcast from decent society. But although a woman was subject to the sanctions of society at large for deviant sexual conduct, her partner in crime was accountable only in person to the man who held property rights in the woman. The law spared the cuckold public shame by leaving him private discretion to respond to the violation of his property according to the economic value that he attached to it. He might or might not bring a private suit against the lover for monetary damages. Common law permitted two such causes of action: one—for "alienation of affections"—gave redress against enticement or abduction of the wife; the other—for "criminal conversation"—vindicated the husband's property right in his wife's body, so that her voluntary participation in the adulterous relation was no defense for her lover. Damages were awarded to compensate the husband for his humiliation and embarrassment, for being deprived of his wife's sexual services, and for the risk of having to provide for children that were not his.[16]

Illegitimate Reproduction

Any sexual activity outside marriage was illicit under the common law, but the gravest threat to the patrilineal family was posed when a child was actually conceived as a result. Sexual misconduct could be concealed, disregarded, or forgotten. Not so a child, whose bodily presence was damning confirmation of moral transgression. The "sin of the flesh" was incarnated in the body of the illegitimate child, who was fatherless in the eyes of the law and as such denied the right to bear his father's name, succeed to his title, or inherit his property. Without affiliation to a male bloodline, he was a political nonentity, a *filius nullius*. This term expressed the moral negation of the offspring of illicit sexual relations rather than the mere technical uncertainty as to the identity of the child's father.[17]

The consequences of illegitimacy varied according to the degree of sinfulness that attached to the circumstances of conception, correlating to the degree of the mother's attachment to or independence of a man. A child born in "concubinage" (a stable unmarried relation) fared better than one born from a casual relation with an unmarried woman. Below these were the "adulterous bastard," born to a married woman of a man other than her husband, and the "incestuous bastard," conceived in a relation that came within the prohibited degrees of marriage. Finally, at least in American law, the most irremediable degree of illegitimacy was found in the "miscegenous bastard," in whose conception the blood boundaries of race were crossed.[18]

Reproduction outside marriage was punished in various forms. Branding the potential offspring of illicit sexual relations as illegitimate was probably the most effective deterrent. A woman had no power to change the child's status—the social position of both was wholly at the mercy of a man. As an act of grace he might legitimate the child by marrying the mother. If he could not or did not wish to marry her, he might yet acknowledge his bastard son for purposes of inheritance, especially in the absence of other legitimate heirs. But these matters lay beyond the woman's control.

Since the man's sexual transgression could not easily be detected (or could be refuted simply by committing perjury), the unmarried mother bore the brunt of punishment. The church regarded her as the root of all deviance from its code of sexual morality and penalized her proportionately. In medieval times in England, the unwed mother was often required to confess her sin in public, after which she might be whipped or placed in the stocks. Infanticide was a measure of last resort for the unwed mother, but punishment for that crime was even more horrible, including sacking (being sewn in a sack and thrown into water), impalement (having a pointed stick driven through the heart), and being buried or burned alive.[19]

During the latter part of the nineteenth century maternity homes were established in the United States to shelter pregnant women. A sincere desire to protect the unmarried mother in her vulnerable situation motivated these social-assistance programs. At the same time they were intended to rehabilitate the "fallen woman" through her moral redemption. The strict disciplinary regime within these institutions was also a form of penalization. Women were forbidden to leave the shelter, subjected to heavy work routines, denied contact with the fathers and the babies, and forced to remain in the shelter for months after giving birth.[20]

Such humiliating and punitive attitudes continue to prevail in contemporary social welfare laws in the United States. The modern state has assumed a measure of responsibility for the welfare of its poor, and the unmarried mother and her child have always been consigned to poverty. However, moral prejudice expresses itself in a reluctance to assist them financially because to do so implies that society condones sin. Concern for the aid recipient's personal morality results in a focus on the woman's sexual activity. For example, Title IV of the U.S. federal Social Security Act of 1935 provided for financial aid to families with dependent children regardless of their parents' marital status. But assistance to illegitimate children was seen as a reward for the mother's immorality. A woman's sexual misconduct, therefore, was and remains cause for denial of public assistance to her child. Under the substitute-father rule, aid has been denied to a child whose mother had sexual relations with any man even outside the home. Extramarital cohabitation, under the man in the house rule, similarly provides grounds to ignore the child's financial needs. The ostensible rationale is that if the mother has a relationship with a man he is to be held accountable for the child's support. In effect, however, these rules are misused so as to penalize the unmarried woman for her sexual activity.[21]

Although social acceptance of single mothers seems to have grown over the past two decades, traces of past stigmatization are still evident. The stereotype of the "unwed mother" is the polar opposite of the "good woman." She is poor and ignorant, promiscuous and oversexed, ungovernable, or unable to act in her own interest. This image is unfounded in reality: most documented illegitimate births occur in the context of ordinary dating relationships and are not a specifically lower-class phenomenon. No comparable deviance label exists for the unmarried father, nor is he considered as crucial a social problem or as important a research subject as his female counterpart.[22]

In spite of a recent trend to equalize the status of the illegitimate and legitimate child, moreover, the consequences of illegitimacy for the child are more extensive today than ever as the law has recognized more and more of the legitimate child's rights against parents and society at large. In common law the chief distinction between legitimate and illegitimate children concerned rights of inheritance.

Illegitimacy in the twentieth century affects a much broader set of legal interests, including custody, guardianship, adoption, birth records, workers' compensation, state and private pensions, inheritance and gift taxes, citizenship, and federal welfare laws.[23]

The Paternity Action

One response to the social problem of out-of-wedlock children in Western countries has been to demand that the father be held financially responsible for his child. This is accomplished by means of legal paternity proceedings. The bastardy action, as it was originally called in common law jurisdictions, was a statutory criminal action designed to remove the burden of supporting the child from local welfare authorities. The first such statute, enacted in England in 1576, was concerned with "bastards being now left to be kept at the charges of the parish where they be born, to the great burden of the same parish . . . and to the evil example and encouragement of the lewd life." Its express purpose was "as well for the punishment of the mother and reputed father of such bastard child, as also for the better relief of every such parish." The paternity action later came to be viewed as a civil proceeding, but in many U.S. jurisdictions it may still be brought by public welfare authorities. In any event, even in such cases the mother is the key witness, and for all practical purposes she bears the burden of proving the man's paternity ("beyond reasonable doubt" in a criminal action or "by a preponderance of the evidence" in a civil action). The man is assumed not to be the child's father unless the mother raises her burden of proof.

Until the fairly recent development of blood testing for paternity, the mother's sexual conduct was a central issue in these actions. The main defense was the *exceptio plurium concubentium*, according to which the action was barred without further ado if it were shown that the mother had had sexual relations with other men at about the time the child was conceived. It appears that it was originally sufficient to produce evidence of the mother's general unchastity. In effect, this amounted to an invitation to the alleged father to commit perjury with a friend who, if subsequently charged with paternity, could invoke the same defense.[24]

Even though an extramarital pregnancy typically occurs in an ordinary dating relationship, paternity actions are brought in only a small fraction of the hundreds of thousands of illegitimate births each year. In the best of circumstances litigation consumes money, time, and energy without any assured outcome. The public examination of the mother's sexual life is humiliating. In some cases there will be pressure from her family to keep the matter secret. In any event, the stigma has a profound effect on the psychology of the mother herself, who tends to assume the full blame and responsibility for her situation. If she retains her self-dignity or, for that matter, any sentiment for the relationship in which her child was conceived, she will wish to preserve her privacy rather than submit to a degrading legal procedure.[25] Finally, even if paternity is established, it is virtually impossible to collect child support from an unwilling father on a regular, long-term basis.

The development of scientific methods to ascertain paternity through blood tests has had little effect on the nature of these legal proceedings. The common approach is that these tests do not show positive proof of a father-child relation but rather exclude the possibility of paternity. The blood of the child, mother, and alleged father is tested for the presence of markers of inherited genes. If, for example, the child's blood contains a marker of which there is no trace in either the mother or the alleged father, one must conclude that it was inherited from someone else and paternity is excluded. Testing for all identifiable genetic factors establishes a probability of exclusion of about 95 percent for a man selected at random from the general population. This does not mean that there is a 5 percent likelihood of paternity for a nonexcluded man but that the child's father will be found among the nonexcluded 5 percent of the general population. If the relevant population is defined by the mother's place of residence in a city with two million males past the age of puberty, a 95 percent probability of exclusion leaves 5 percent of the population (one hundred thousand males) as possible fathers. On the basis of this calculation alone, the likelihood of paternity for any nonexcluded man is only one in a hundred thousand.[26]

This approach does not, however, take into account that an alleged father is not selected at random from the general male population but within the context of the mother's social relations. Once a man has been identified by the mother as the father of her child, the specific genetic constitutions of the triad provide data from which a likelihood of paternity can be calculated to a high degree of accuracy. Even if evidence about the mother's sexual relations indicates more than one possible father, comparison of the results obtained from blood typing of those men can establish who is more likely to be the father. Statistical formulas that compute the test results, together with all other nonquantitative evidence presented in a given case, including the weight attached to the mother's testimony, can thus produce a high likelihood of paternity that may approximate certainty.

Yet the use of blood tests to prove paternity remains controversial. Aside from questions about the scientific reliability of blood-typing data and the competence of testing facilities, there is concern about false accusations and frivolous paternity suits. Given that the insurmountable element of human fallibility always leaves a margin of scientific doubt, this skepticism seems to reflect old prejudices about the character of the woman bringing the action.[27] The focus on the marginal possibility of not excluding a falsely accused man appears to presuppose that the mother's allegation of paternity is unfounded because she is either promiscuous or a liar. Indeed, it is astounding that the "typical fact pattern in paternity litigation" can still be presented in terms of a woman who "has had sexual relations with approximately equal frequency with each of three men and only these three during the time period in which conception almost surely occurred."[28] The focus on the possibility of false allegations brings to mind the bias that the rape victim is a temptress and a liar.

In this context the question of the value of blood-typing data is posed with the purpose of absolving a man from responsibility for a child that is not his. If, however, the blood tests are undertaken with the purpose of assuming responsibility for a child and on the assumption that the mother's testimony is truthful, the blood data would appear to provide a high degree of certainty in biological paternity. In other words, if the alleged father is intent on evading parental responsibility, the margin of uncertainty inherent in the scientific tests will be emphasized; whereas if his prior intent is to claim the child as his biological offspring, the margin of doubt may be accepted as negligible.

In its present form, the paternity action in the United States is a legal arena in which the welfare authority and the putative father as the adversaries pit their wits in an attempt to evade responsibility for the illegitimate child at the expense of the mother's social reputation and the child's welfare. But blood tests can establish a likelihood of paternity that is at least comparable to (if not more precise than) the probability assumed in the case of a child born within marriage. Paternity actions could be conducted in a manner radically different from the present procedure if blood test findings were interpreted in an atmosphere that gave due credit to the mother's testimony and imposed the burden of proof on the alleged father. In several European countries, for example, the legal proceeding is now based on a presumption of paternity rather than nonpaternity.[29] A man who wishes to evade responsibility for a child might refute the presumption and raise his burden of proving nonpaternity by identifying another man who is more likely to be the father.

Choice and Responsibility

All this clearly establishes a double standard of reproductive conduct, which complements that of sexual morality, according to which women bear responsibility for rearing children and men do not. Indeed, the norm of paternal irresponsibility underlies the statutory discrimination of unmarried fathers in relation to unmarried mothers, some instances of which have been challenged in recent years in the United States.

In *Stanley v. Illinois* (1972),[30] for example, the U.S. Supreme Court declared unconstitutional a statute that automatically conferred guardianship of illegitimate children to the state on the mother's death without giving the father a right to a hearing on his parental fitness. In *Ca-*

ban v. Mohammed (1979)[31] the court struck down a statute that required consent of the unmarried mother, but not of the unmarried father, to the adoption of their illegitimate child.[32] In *Parham v. Hughes* (1979),[33] however, the court rejected an equal-protection challenge to a tort statute under which unmarried mothers, but not fathers, were allowed to seek monetary compensation for the wrongful death of an illegitimate child. The court justified the statute's disparate treatment as reflecting real biological differences between men and women, including the uncertainty of paternity.

Biology is easily cited as grounds for a double standard of parental responsibility. The clear biological connection between mother and child is seen to give rise naturally to the mother's "unshakable responsibility for the care of the child,"[34] while the relation between father and child is a matter of the man's choosing to grasp "an opportunity no other male possesses to develop a relationship with his offspring."[35]

Although it is true that women and not men care for their children (a norm that probably originates in the uncertainty of biological paternity), parental responsibility is the social activity of an independent moral agent and is not dictated by biological sex. If mothering is portrayed as biological destiny, it is a contradiction in terms to attach moral value and social worth to women's nurturing of children. If we continue to use the uncertainty of paternity as an excuse to absolve men from responsibility for their children, we perpetuate the double standard. When courts of law justify sex-based classifications by referring to the cultural norm of paternal irresponsibility and by presuming that fathers are unidentified and absent, it is more likely that these generalizations will continue to be true.[36]

CHAPTER 3
Adoption

But it touched my heart so forcibly to think of parting
entirely with the child, and, for aught I knew, of having it
murdered, or starved by neglect and ill-usage (which was
much the same), that I could not think of it without horror.
I wish all those women who consent to the disposing their
children out of the way, as it is called, for decency sake,
would consider that 'tis only a contrived method for
murder; that is to say, a-killing their children with safety.
—*Daniel Defoe,* Moll Flanders

The Family as Fiction

In ancient times the patriarchal family, not the individual, formed
the fundamental social unit. The general belief was that society was
a collection of persons united by common descent from the progen-
itor of an original family. At the same time stories were known of
men of alien descent who had been admitted to the original broth-
erhood. The contradiction between the belief in the natural origins
of the political entity and the knowledge of its artificial composition
was reconciled in the legal fiction of adoption, which permitted family relations to be created artificially. In theory political membership
was attainable only through blood connection, but the family was
constantly enlarged by the adoption of strangers within its circle.
This fiction seems to have been essential in broadening the scope of
political organization beyond the circles of biological kinship.[1]

Roman law recognized two forms of adoption: full and simple.
Full adoption (*adrogatio*) was designed to save a family line from
extinction and replaced the adoptee's previous ancestor cult with the
adopter's. Since the power of the head of the family, the *patria potestas,* was absolute and inalienable, this form of adoption was pos-

sibly only in regard to someone who was not subject to the power of another male head of family (*paterfamilias*). Simple adoption (*adoptio*), by contrast, could establish a familial relation between an adopter with heirs of his own and an adoptee subject to the power of his own paterfamilias. It actually terminated one potestas to create a new one. A poor family could improve a child's lot by having the child adopted upward into a rich heirless family. Through adoption a man could also legitimate a child from a concubine.[2]

Adoption was not known in common law. It was introduced by statute in the United States in the mid-nineteenth century as a result of social concern for the plight of the illegitimate child and the political pressure of middle-class childless couples. Social conditions were conducive to new adoption laws: a fluid social system, an underpopulated country, and an ideology that a man was not simply born into his rank but created his own place in the world. Patrilineal status was of declining significance in a democratic, industrial society. The property system of land-holding based on blood lines, a legacy from feudal times, was giving way to a market of liquid capital. Urbanization with its industrial slums gave a new dimension to the problem of mothers and children in poverty. Modern psychology and liberal philosophy brought concern for the welfare of children and the notion that they could be subjects of rights. Woman's shrinking domestic role and a cult of romanticized motherhood produced a new interest in legal adoption on the part of childless nonworking women, who pressured for permanent, exclusive parental rights. Finally, adoption was perceived as putting fewer demands on state coffers than either foster or institutional care.[3]

Before the passage of the first adoption statute in 1851, destitute children were provided for under the colonial American poor laws. Like their English counterparts, these laws were punitive in character, reflecting the belief that the poor were eager to abandon their children and avoid responsibility for their support at the expense of the local parish. Poverty as such served as a ground for depriving parents of custody of their children. The common method of providing long-term care for indigent children during the nineteenth century in the United States was indenture, supplemented by the poorhouse. Indenture meant that the child was lodged with a pioneer farming family and worked for his keep as an apprentice. This provided the employer with free labor without affording the child any protection against abuse or neglect. In the poorhouses children worked under conditions that often approached those of a reformatory rather than a family home.[4]

Concern for the welfare of uncared-for children was a central theme in the resulting legal regulation of adoption. The typical adoptee was born out of wedlock to a mother who possessed neither the economic ability nor the social support necessary to raise her child. Adoption would rescue the child from destitution and afford a caring, stable home environment while erasing the stigma of illegitimacy. As opposed to indenture, it involved some screening of the adoptive family. To give the child a fresh start in life, the link to the birth family was completely severed. This also insulated the adoptive family from the supposedly immoral influence of the birth parents, or their blackmail and harassment. Such fears of the birth parents derived largely from class prejudice against the poor.[5]

Passage of the adoption acts was opposed on the moralistic grounds that their effect would be to condone extramarital sexual activity and relieve unmarried mothers from stigma, punishment, and responsibility for their conceived-in-sin children. To all appearances these moralisms were outweighed by the enlightened desire to give unfortunate children a new start in life, unencumbered by the circumstances of their births. In fact, however, penalizing attitudes toward the relinquishing birth mother persisted in the new system.

Illegitimate Motherhood

We have already seen how the stereotype of the out-of-wedlock mother as a promiscuous woman is a reaction to the threat she poses to the sexual order of patriarchal society. This imagery is reinforced by an adoption system that obscures the birth mother's real identity through its final and irreversible severance of her ties with the child. Secrecy and anonymity in adoption were seen as a means not only to protect the adoptive family but to conceal the affront to moral convention posed by extramarital reproduction. Illegitimate pregnancies were hidden by removing the women from their regular environments to special maternity homes. Seclusion in these homes was a measure taken by the community in self-protection against the mothers' negative influence, much as primitive societies provided isolation huts to prevent menstruating women from contaminating their villages. Even today the unwed pregnant (white) teenager drops out of school and becomes an outsider shrouded in horror and mystery.[6]

The image of the "red-haired floozie" informs the fantasies of adopted girls about their birth mothers. Emotionally disordered adolescents have a tendency to become pregnant, as if acting out the role of the whore mother.[7] Even the unwed mothers themselves fall victim to the whore stereotype:

> I was almost as scared about going to the Home as I was in telling my parents that I was pregnant. Because I had a preconceived idea that it would be run like an Institution, in that all the girls in the Home would be sluts and they'd give me a hard time. No, I didn't identify with the other girls! Because I wasn't one of them. I was a nice girl. . . . The Matron came in and we chatted, and my mother tried to show her what a nice, Christian girl I was, that I'd been to Sunday School, that I was educated, that I was actually a schoolteacher and that the father and I had been in love and that we had been engaged. . . . We still didn't think—realise—that we'd actually encountered some of these dreadful sluts we'd been fearing. They were actually the nice girls that were making cups of tea and popping in and out all the time.[8]

One major study in the 1950s explained out-of-wedlock pregnancy as a psychological pathology. It was the consequence of a purposeful act, motivated by the mother's neurotic desire to have sole possession of a baby outside a normal, mating love relation. The unmarried mother was so absorbed in her pathetic drama that she was truly unable to comprehend the separate needs of her child. She needed professional help to make the right decision for the child's future, to surrender him or her in adoption to a mature married couple who would be able to care for the child properly.[9]

In reality, sexual activity and failure in contraception account for most unplanned pregnancies, and the birth mother comes from all layers and segments of society (including married women).[10] The taboo and stigma of the relinquishing birth mother are social constructs that reflect the norm of reproduction within marriage. The norm is universal; it cuts across class, race, and religion. Its violation defines the woman as an unfit mother, leaving her no real choice but to relinquish her child.

The birth mother strikes a bargain with society, for by doing the best for her child she can restore her own virtue. The primary objective of adoption is to legitimate the child. The counseling given by social workers is clear: the mother should forget her own selfish needs and give the child a new, better life unmarked by the stigma of illegitimacy. Once the child is surrendered, the mother's sin is exorcised and her virtue reinstated.[11]

The social desire to erase all traces of the sin of illegitimacy tends to override the independent wishes of the unwed mother and to exert pressure on her at a time of heightened vulnerability. There is a tacit assumption that she will consent to adoption. The expectation that she will do so undermines her confidence in her ability to parent her own child, precisely when she needs emotional support to face her tenuous social and financial situation.[12] "Nobody said, 'Do you want to keep the baby?' I don't think *ever*."[13]

Pressure to surrender the infant continues after its birth. The widespread belief in maternal instinct seems not to hold under these circumstances.[14] Counseling is clearly biased toward discouraging the unwed mother from keeping her child. Social workers not uncommonly advise the expectant mother not to see her baby after birth. They fear that contact with the baby will make relinquishment harder and induce the mother to change her mind.[15] Thus, in practice, the mother-child relationship is severed at birth, even before she officially consents to adoption and the legal termination of her parental rights. The actual consent is often given in an impersonal bureaucratic atmosphere with the papers already filled out and ready for signature. Some women so suppress their experience of surrender that they cannot recall a single detail.[16]

The culture that stigmatizes the unwed mother simultaneously affirms the virtue of motherhood. The relinquishment of a child would be considered "unnatural" in a married woman, an evasion of her cultural or sociobiological destiny as mother and a rejection of her child. As a result, the promise of exorcised sin is not realized for the relinquishing birth mother because her act constitutes a new unforgivable and unforgettable sin. She may start afresh to become a devout churchgoer, a devoted wife and a pillar of the community, but always there lurks the fear that someone will uncover her sordid past and brand her as the sinner she really is.[17]

In fact relinquishment is not usually a rejection as such but rather a consequence of a combination of objective factors, including youth, poverty, and lack of social support to keep the child. Public opinion of illegitimacy and social security provisions appear to determine rates of relinquishment.[18] In Sweden, for example, where the attitude toward sexual activity is liberal and where the state provides adequate child care services and women's salaries more nearly equal those of men than in any other country, scarcely a hundred children a year are given up for adoption.[19] Indeed, moralistic judgment of illegitimate pregnancy is deeply embedded in the legal structure of adoption.

Closed Adoption

In U.S. law, adoption is generally effected by a two-tier judicial process in which termination of the birth parents' rights precedes and is separate from the establishment of the adoptive parents' legal relation to the child. At both stages of the process the court hearings are held behind closed doors. On issuing the final adoption decree all papers and records pertaining to the birth family and the circumstances of surrender, including the child's original birth certificate, are sealed. Finally the child is given legal rebirth in the adoptive family by the issuance of a new birth certificate in which the names of the adoptive parents are substituted for those of the birth parents.

Rules governing the subsequent release of information about the procedure vary from state to state, but access to the original birth certificate and court records is generally allowed only by special court order on showing of good cause.[20] The courts apply this discretionary standard quite strictly, requiring proof of mild or severe psychological need on the part of the adoptee, together with evidence of his or her maturity and the consent of both the birth and the adoptive parents. Access to sealed records is not allowed on grounds of psychological need alone, or mere curiosity.[21]

Closed hearings and sealed records guarantee the confidentiality of the act of adoption. The two-tier process that separates the termination of the legal parent-child relation in the biological family and its establishment in the nonbiological family further insures mutual anonymity of the birth and adoptive parents. The policy of secrecy is rationalized as serving the interests of all the involved parties: the adoptee is protected from any possible stigma of illegitimacy, the adoptive parents can develop a relationship to the child without the threat of interference from the birth parents, and the birth mother has a chance to make a new life for herself without fear of her past being revealed.[22] At the same time it buries all traces of a biological family connection that is considered sinful and shameful. The slates are wiped clean in the legal rebirth of the child in the adoptive family.

Changes in social attitudes to extramarital reproduction and single parenthood have, however, resulted in a questioning of the need for complete anonymity in adoption and its desirability.[23] Much of the criticism of the closed system of adoption has come from adult adoptees in search of their origins, claiming a right to know. Their searches have revealed the birth mothers, who in turn may question the assumptions about their interests in closed adoption.

Taboo and Fear of the Unknown

The legal rebirth of the adopted child is enacted in the adoptive family by the pretense that she or he belongs to that family on all levels, not just the social-psychological one, and that the child never had any other parents. Inherent in the adoption process is the symbolic death of the birth parents, which renders them taboo.[24] The silence in this fiction has two tones. It often conceals the adoptive parents' unresolved feelings of inadequacy because of their infertility and their fear of losing the child to the 'real' parents. Yet it represses the specter of illegitimacy, the 'dirty little secret' of the child's assumed origin in sexual promiscuity. What is more, the secrecy of adoption exposes the adoptee to the risk of violating yet another taboo—incest. Whatever the statistical probability of sexual encounter with a blood relative, the adopted person's unknowing susceptibility to incest adds a unique psychological dimension to his or her social situation.[25]

In recent years, professionals have been advising adoptive parents to tell their children about the adoption at a young age as part of their responsibility for childhood sex education.[26] The four-year-old girl who asks how babies are made is actually asking a question about herself. If the answer is kept secret, the message conveyed in the embarrassed silence is that there is something unspeakable about the child herself. This leaves an emotional imprint of alienation and rejection. There will also be a subtle effect on the cognitive development of the child, who learns that there are questions—touching on the essence of her very being—which ought not be asked and that the impulse to know must be suppressed.

Secrecy affects the adoptee's relationship with the adoptive and birth families in other ways, too. The pretense that the adoptive family is just like any other denies reality. Various situational discrepancies exist between adoptive and biological parenthood, including the emotional difficulty of involuntary childlessness, the need to demonstrate parental eligibility to adoption authorities, the lack of emotional preparation for parenthood through the period of pregnancy, the insecurity of parental status pending finalization of the adoption decree, and the absence of external signs (such as maternity clothing) and rites of passage to mark the child's arrival and the transition into the role of parents.[27] The different reality of adoptive parenthood is echoed in the popular sentiment that adoptive kinship is somehow inferior to biological kinship, a bias closely associated with derogatory attitudes to both illegitimacy and infertility. If the adoptive parents are unable to acknowledge this difference they are likely to be inhibited in their capacity to communicate and empathize with the child in relation to the child's special social situation.

At the same time the adoptee's relation to the birth family takes place in the realm of fantasy and fear of the unknown. In a state of ignorance, the child is apt either to idealize the birth parents or exaggerate their faults. The first fantasy can impede the forming of a real ongoing relationship with the adoptive parents. The second can result in low self-esteem due to internalization of characteristics that are imagined to be hereditary.[28]

It is commonly understood today that a biological connection is not necessary to the psychological parent-child relation. Rather than being a matter of blood relationship, parenting is seen as a social activity of daily care and response to the child's physical and emotional needs, as a result of which the child forms a psychological attachment to the caretaking adult. Even the most loved adopted children, however, may have persistent feelings of rejection and alienation and wish to have information about their biological parents.[29]

The identity of biological kin—parents, grandparents, aunts, uncles, and siblings—is taken for granted by nonadopted persons, but in closed adoption knowledge of such genealogy is lacking. This tends to cause confusion and uncertainty for the adoptee in adolescence, a developmental stage in which self-identity forms through a vacillating process of identification with and individuation from the parents. Individuation, or detachment, is accompanied by a sense of loss and isolation. The adoptee's actual experience of loss of birth parents makes him or her particularly vulnerable to any additional experience of rejection.

Adolescence also marks puberty and the emergence of a sexual-reproductive consciousness that is accompanied by an awareness of the biological continuity of generations. Absent knowledge of the birth family, the adoptee's sense of biological connectedness contains a void. The adoptee may have concern about the transmission of hereditary traits to offspring or fears of unknowing incest. Teenage pregnancy—which is generally a means of individuation and of gaining adult status—might serve also to compensate an adoptee for a sense of biological unrootedness, providing a first contact with a blood relative.[30]

The artificial severance of the birth family leaves the adoptee anonymous and unattached. The psychological isolation of being unrelated to any other person is profound. The anonymous child has no point of reference; she or he is always out of context. In adulthood, life-cycle events—such as marriage or divorce, birth of a child, death of an adoptive parent—are likely to precipitate a search for the birth parents.[31]

The adoptee's search for biological origins is often taken by the adoptive parents to reflect their own failure or inadequacy as parents. They fear that a successful search will result in a transfer of the child's affections to the birth parents and a rejection of themselves. But the evidence contradicts such fears. The search seems to imply that blood is thicker than love, but it is really a response and challenge to the conspiracy of silence around adoption. The adoptee's curiosity about his or her biological origins is a quest for self-knowledge rather than for new-old parents. Research has shown that a successful search for the birth family does not endanger the adoptive family. On the contrary, it may often have a positive effect on the adoptive relationship because the adoptee's enhanced self-identity is likely to reinforce the psychological parent-child attachment in the adoptive family.[32]

A study of fifty randomly selected cases of reunions between adult adoptees and their birth parents concluded that the reunion had some enhancing effect on the adoptive relationship, regardless of the relationship that had existed previously between adoptee and adoptive parents. Even where an ongoing relationship between adoptee and birth parents developed because of the reunion, the adoptee came to realize that the psychological relationship with the adoptive parents was far more important than a new connection with the birth parents. And when the adoptive parents' feared loss did not materialize, they were relieved and reassured of the strength of their relation to the adoptee.[33]

Similarly, research findings refute the assumption, never substantiated with information offered by birth mothers themselves, that the birth mother's primary interest is to maintain secrecy. Indeed, confidentiality precluded any gathering of such information, since that would necessarily intrude on the woman's privacy. Secrecy was supposed to afford the birth mother a new start in life, unblemished by the sin and shame of her past. It was assumed that she surrendered the child in reliance on a promise of anonymity and wanted only to be left alone. But as a result of this protectionist policy the birth mothers were ignored, forgotten and silenced in the aftermath of relinquishment.

Although the psychology of the birth mother during pregnancy and relinquishment had been researched, the first follow-up study was undertaken only in the mid-1970s, inspired by an adult adoptee whose search for his biological parents was obstructed by an adoption agency policy that prohibited any participation in reunions. The researchers stated that the primary goal of their study was to give the birth parents an opportunity to speak for themselves, to express their own feelings and needs.

To avoid any invasion of privacy, contact was established through publicity about the research. Hundreds of letters from birth parents of all ages were received, many of the respondents volunteering to be directly involved in the study. Thirty-eight birth parents (thirty-six female and two male) were then contacted and personally interviewed. The findings were as follows:

- 76 percent of the interviewees had been married at least once since the relinquishment, and of these 86 percent reported they had told their spouses of the adoption;
- 82 percent said they would be interested in a reunion, if the adoptee desired to meet them and if he or she had reached adulthood;
- 87 percent stated they had no wish to hurt the adoptive parents; none visualized the development of an actual parental relationship;
- 95 percent affirmed that they were interested in updating the information concerning them in agency case records;

- 53 percent were in favor of opening sealed records to adult adoptees, and 80 percent of establishing mediating boards to assist in reunions;
- 50 percent said that they continued to have feelings of loss, pain, and mourning over the child they had relinquished, after a median interval of fifteen years since the adoption.[34]

The total severance of the biological parent-child relation in closed adoption allows the child to be legally reborn, but conversely, the elimination of the birth parents' names from the official new birth certificate amounts to their legal death. The emotional experience of relinquishment under such conditions is tantamount to losing a child in death. The grief that accompanies such a loss is suppressed and remains unresolved when the adoption system operates on the assumption that the birth mother is concerned mainly with the pretense of a fresh start in life.[35]

Subsequent studies have produced similar findings as regards the willingnesss of birth parents to participate in reunions with adoptees.[36] The assumption that the birth mother is primarily interested in forgetting and concealing her past appears to be a misconception. In most cases she relinquishes her baby to secure for it a caring home situation that she cannot provide. Her greatest concern is that the child will never forgive her for abandoning him or her.[37]

Open Adoption

Closed adoption systems operate mainly through licensed agencies that have exclusive access to information relating to the parties involved and control of its dissemination. The agency also has total authority as to the child's placement. In the interim period between termination of the birth parents' rights and finalization of the adoption decree, the agency has actual legal custody of the child. The termination of parental rights and the agency's subsequent assumption of the custodial role mark the end of the birth parents' control over the child's future. They have no say in selecting the adoptive family and are excluded, by the policy of secrecy and anonymity, from all future knowledge about the child.

The adult adoptee's assertion of a right to know is not addressed to the adoptive parents but rather to this system of closed adoption and sealed records. Obviously, adoptive parents cannot impart to their children information that they do not already have. But attempts to challenge the constitutionality of sealed records statutes and good cause standards of disclosure have been unsuccessful. The right to know has been formulated as a matter of equal protection, since adoptees and nonadoptees are treated differentially regarding access to information about biological kin. First amendment rights to receive information, and a right of privacy with respect to genealogical information necessary to reproductive decisions, have also been suggested. However, the courts have consistently dismissed these arguments in light of countervailing interests also found to merit constitutional protection. The adoptive parents are said to have a right to confidentiality and to familial integrity, supported by the state's interest in promoting a stable home environment for the adopted child. The birth mother is said to have a right to privacy, encompassing the right to be let alone, the right to choose—as a matter of reproductive freedom—to surrender the child for adoption rather than rear the child herself, and the right to confidentiality in personal matters pertaining to intimate sexual relationships.[38]

Although the courts have insisted on mainintaing secrecy as a matter of policy, changing attitudes toward marriage, divorce, and extramarital pregnancy have affected actual practice in the new notion of "open" adoption. The greater social acceptance of unwed mothers has brought with it a reluctance to surrender parental rights through adoption because that entails severing the relationship with the child. Nevertheless, single mothers often find themselves in economic circumstances that make it difficult to care adequately for the child. Open adoption affords the birth parent an active role in finding a satisfactory home for the child and in deciding to what extent—if at all—there will be ongoing contact with the adoptive family. It rejects both the secrecy of the conventional model of adoption and the severance of the adoptee's ties with the birth family. The adoptive and birth parents have full access to information about each other and mutually select each other, reclaiming the power and control vested in the agency under the system of closed adoption.[39] In open adoption the birth parent meets the adoptive parents and retains the right to continuing contact and knowledge of the child's whereabouts and welfare, but at the same time she relinquishes all legal and moral rights to care and custody of the child.[40]

Open adoption has been suggested as a solution to the problem of "foster care drift," in which a child passes through a series of foster homes and institutions because the birth parents refuse to terminate their parental rights and foster parents are unwilling to assume permanent responsibility without legal protection of their relationship with the child. The lack of continuous, stable parenting is associated with higher rates of juvenile delinquence and psychological disturbance in the child.[41] In a variation on open adoption, foster parents may be vested with rights of custody while birth parents retain visitation rights, as after a divorce. Studies of such arrangements have uniformly found that continued contact with the birth parents had a positive effect, promoting the child's sense of well-being and emotional security, even where the birth parents were irresponsible and contact was sporadic, tenuous, and infrequent.[42] Similarly, in several instances courts have awarded permanent custody rights to persons other than birth parents with visitation rights to members of the birth family.[43] Finally, the Model State Adoption Act (1980) allows the parties involved in adoption to avoid the secrecy surrounding relinquishment and the mutual isolation of birth and adoptive families by entering a written agreement, to be approved by a court, that permits continuing contact of the birth relatives with the child and the adoptive parents.[44]

Open adoption is usually effected through so-called independent or private placement, to be distinguished from the principle mechanism for adoption in U.S. law—that of "public" or "agency" placement. Public adoption is controlled by the state through licensed agencies. On the birth parents' voluntary termination of parental rights the agency places the child with a prospective adoptive family that has been screened for fitness or suitability. The adoption is finalized by court decree within several months, after the findings of a home study prove satisfactory. Private adoption, by contrast, is effectuated by unlicensed intermediaries, most often through the connection of the pregnant woman's physician with an attorney who finds an adoptive home and makes the legal arrangements. The child is likely to be placed immediately with adoptive parents, whereas agency placement often entails interim foster care. Although here, too, the court will order a home study before it issues the final adoption decree, there are no known criteria for eligibility of adoptive parents. The standard applied focuses on minimum requirements rather than on "the best suitable home," and courts are reluctant to remove children from less than adequate homes once they have been placed. Nevertheless, there is little evidence that independent placement is less successful than agency placement in terms of the child's welfare.[45]

Independent placement has advantages over the agency process. The birth and adoptive parents are more likely to have information about each other. Prospective adoptive parents can avoid bureaucratic delays in the agency application process and in the completion of preplacement home studies and can sidestep screening criteria that they perceive as arbitrary or inappropriate (such as length of marriage, age, infertility, working status of adoptive mother, minimum income, religion). Many birth mothers find that private adoption offers preferable financial assistance with respect to medical care, housing, and living expenses, whereas licensed agencies are bureaucratic and impersonal.[46]

The Black Market in Babies

At the same time independent placement has certain disadvantages, including the danger of commercialization, which is particularly pertinent to the legal discussion of surrogate mother agreements. Whereas the quality of agency placement services is subject to state control through licensing requirements, independent placement is more susceptible to the influence of economic market factors and entails a risk of profit-making by the private intermediary. The un-licensed go-between might pressure the birth mother to surrender her child and charge the adoptive parents exorbitant fees in exchange for the child they covet. In other words, the danger is that the self-interest of the profiteer, rather than concern for the interests of the child and the birth and adoptive parents, will motivate the adoption process.

This fear of exploitation by "baby brokers" engenders the public policy against baby selling, which is expressed in legislation that regulates the payment of fees in connection with adoption place-ment. Although many states make no provision in this respect, some juridictions do not allow independent placement and prohibit pay-ment of any compensation except to a licensed agency. Adoption placements that contravene this prohibition take place in a black market in babies.[47] Other states regulate placement fees by requiring an itemized report of all charges and expenditures for court or state department approval and by stipulating the kinds of fees that may be paid (such as birth-related medical expenses and legal costs incurred in the adoption process). Violations of these restrictions constitute a gray market in adoption.

Illegal adoption activity results from an unsatisfied demand for adoptable children (healthy white newborns) with increasing infer-tility rates among middle-class couples and strict criteria for parental eligibility with formidable waiting lists in adoption agencies. At the same time the supply of babies is diminished due to widespread use of contraceptives, liberalization of abortion laws, and the fading so-cial stigma attaching to unmarried mothers. In its most extreme form black market adoption bypasses the legal process of adoption en-tirely, in that the birth mother registers falsely at the hospital under the adoptive mother's name.[48] The price of a baby on the black mar-ket is reported to range from four to forty thousand dollars. Most of the profits appear to be gathered by the intermediary doctors and lawyers, rather than the mothers who bear the children.[49]

The more common mode of illegal placement—in the gray mar-ket—is less blatant, involving an under-the-table passage of money from the adoptive parents to the intermediary. The parties agree to disclose only that portion of the fee pertaining to allowable professional services, and the illegal sum is paid in cash. This arrangement is unlikely to be detected. First, it is difficult to distinguish between fees for professional services and money paid in connection with placement. Second, the exploited parties are unlikely to share relevant information: the birth mother is often ignorant of the transaction; and though the adoptive parents might have cause to complain, they would probably not air their grievance for fear of losing the child.[50]

Attributing the black market to a shortage in the supply of adoptable babies can lead to the conclusion that the market may be controlled or eliminated by addressing criminal norms to those who create the demand. Criminal liability for violation of the ban against baby bartering is normally applied to the recipient of an illegal payment, but it could be extended to the prospective adoptive parents, too. However, further criminalization would probably merely entrench the underground nature of the activity. In economic terms, increasing the risk of unpleasant consequences merely raises the cost of production where the demand is more or less set. Inasmuch as the problem is akin to prohibiting alcohol and drug sales, or prostitution, the more effective remedy might be to provide to infertile couples readily available and satisfactory legal alternatives (such as surrogate mother arrangements and other variations on reproductive technology).[51] If the problem is one of unscrupulous practices by profiteering intermediaries, the solution is to improve the position of the exploited persons. An essential element in the power of the intermediary is the information that he or she holds about the identity of the involved parties. Arguably, opening the adoption process and allowing personal contact between the parties would reduce their vulnerability, enhance their control, and mitigate the intermediary's power.

Indeed, all states (including those that prohibit independent placement) allow biological parents to place a child with close relatives without state intervention, which indicates that intermediary activity is the focus of the public policy against selling babies. The risk of profiteering and exploitation is improbable in intrafamily adoption, and it is not at all clear that the baby barter ban applies where the "buyer" is a blood relative. For example, *In re Estate of Shirk* (1960) involved a mother who consented to adoption by the child's maternal grandmother in exchange for a one-third interest in the grand-mother's estate. The court held that this "family compact" did not contravene the public policy that was aimed only at a parent who "attempts to relieve himself from all parental obligation, [by] placing the burden on another who assumes it, without natural affection or moral obligation, . . . only because of the bargain."[52]

The Birth Mother's Consent

But another concern that arises with regard to independent place-ment is that the birth mother will be manipulated by the profiteering intermediary into consenting to the adoption. Even if the pressure does not amount to legal fraud or duress, the truly voluntary nature of her consent may be questioned. In an adoption through an agency this risk is supposedly averted by counseling. Although the services offered by agencies in this respect have been strongly biased from the outset toward adoption as the best solution, the absence of coun-seling for birth mothers is a point often raised in criticism of inde-pendent adoption. The intermediary lawyers and doctors are neither trained to handle the stresses involved in the adoption decision nor legally obligated to inform birth mothers of alternatives to adoption or the availability of professional counseling. Legislative policies that prohibit placement other than through a licensed agency protect the birth mother and her child against irresponsible, careless, and untrained intermediaries as much as against intentional exploitation. According to the Child Welfare League of America's 1977 study of independent adoption, 86 percent of the interviewed birth mothers had considered plans other than adoption, but only 40 percent re-ported discussing alternatives with the intermediary, and only one case was actually referred for counseling.[53]

Mandatory counseling could be prescribed, of course, by legisla-tion. Arguably, legalizing the adoption market together with supportive counseling for the birth mother would remove the conditions that are so conducive to disinterested profiteering and exploitation. But another question, particularly pertinent to surrogacy, remains: whether monetary payment to the birth mother herself rather than to the intermediary should be allowed. The concern is that the financial incentive might induce her to reach a decision she would not have made otherwise and will subsequently regret. This relates not only to the effect of a promise to pay a lump sum on relinquishment, but also to her remuneration for ongoing expenses during pregnancy.

From the birth mother's point of view, independent placement has the advantage that the prospective adoptive parents, through the intermediary, pay for her medical and living expenses beyond the financial assistance available from agencies. But if she wants to change her mind later about surrendering the child she might have to pay back these sums, and since she is unlikely to have the necessary funds, the indebtedness might exert pressure on her to sign a consent to adoption. The fear is that monetary factors will distort the voluntary nature of the birth mother's decision to place her child for adoption.

One may distinguish, however, between the initial decision and the later change of mind. Monetary factors do indeed influence choices, given the economy of the world we all live in. Promise of compensation may increase the range of feasible options; yet once a decision is reached it may become irreversible for all practical purposes. The predicament of the birth mother who cannot afford to refund money she has received does not necessarily reflect on the voluntariness of her initial decision. It arises at a later point at which she wishes to reverse a decision that has not been finalized because of a uniform policy that postpones the legal effect of consent to adoption until after the child's birth.

For example, section 7(a) of the Uniform Adoption Act provides that "consent to adoption shall be executed at any time after the child's birth." And according to section 19(b)(1), voluntary termination of parental rights is not final and may be withdrawn—apparently for any reason—"within 10 days after it is signed or the child is born, whichever is later." The length of the cooling period varies from state to state, but no jurisdiction gives legal effect to *pre*natal consent to adoption or termination of parental rights. This means, in effect, that the birth mother has a legally protected right to change her mind with respect to her initial decision to place her child for adoption. The accepted rationale for this policy is that she cannot fully appreciate the significance of surrender until after the child is born and she has recovered from the immediate trauma of giving birth.[54]

Once consent has been lawfully given, however, it can be revoked only with difficulty. Legislative and judicial policies in this respect are fairly restrictive. Generally speaking, proof of fraud or duress, or at least something more than a mere change of mind, is required to invalidate consent to adoption. This conforms with the general law of obligations and takes into consideration the child's need for stable placement and the adoptive parents' legitimate expectation of finality once they have received the child into their care.[55]

The lenient attitude toward the legally binding effect of consent to adoption is understandable when one considers the drastic consequences of such consent in a system of closed adoption. If the effect of adoption is to sever any connection between the birth parent and child in terms of social contact and means of identification, then due care must be taken to insure that the surrendering parent is fully aware of the meaning of his or her legal act of consent. However, the protectionist policy of the law belies a paternalism that also constrains the autonomy of the person making the decision to relinquish the child.

What is more, this approach seems to stem from a view that characterizes the experience of pregnancy as an emotionally volatile state of being that undermines any rational frame of mind. We have seen that the law's approach to women's reproductive role in the biological family is based on a fundamental notion of the subjectivity of the womb. In the context of adoption this is supplemented by an attitude that the woman cannot fully comprehend the condition of pregnancy until it is rendered concrete by the actual birth of the child and its separate physical presence. It is intimated that this concrete evidence of the woman's situation renders it more conducive to reasoned consideration, as if the expulsion of the baby from the womb signifies an end to the woman's emotional turmoil and contributes, in some inherent way, to the rational resolution of her dilemma whether to keep the child.[56]

Obviously, a child cannot be surrendered for adoption before the birth. It does not follow, however, that the decision itself cannot be finalized before that event. The problematic social dimensions of the birth mother's situation—that is, the absence of material and emotional support for the unwed mother in a cultural context that otherwise reveres motherhood as woman's true fulfillment—are not resolved in any way by the child's birth. Nor is there any guarantee that a decision made within days of childbirth, with all *its* attendant physical and emotional effects, will be a better considered one. In this respect, the policy that delays the binding effect of consent to adoption might merely perpetuate the birth mother's conflicting doubts and aggravate her psychological predicament. Indeed, according to a British study of unmarried mothers, not all of whom gave up their babies, more than four out of five would have preferred to give their consent only once and to have it final as soon as it was given.[57]

Strictly speaking, the policy of postnatal consent is aimed only at the birth mother. Until recently the law did not require consent of unmarried fathers to adoption. Even today section 302 of the Model Adoption Act allows the child's father to sign a relinquishment before the birth, whereas the mother must wait until seventy-two hours thereafter.[58] What is more, as we shall see in the next chapter, when a man donates sperm to be used in artificial insemination to establish a nonbiological family, he is automatically divested of his parental rights, and the general law of the artificial insemination family is tantamount to a scheme of prior-to-conception consent to adoption.

CHAPTER 4

Artificial Insemination:
Secrecy and Anonymity

A begotten God, the Jews say, must logically have a
mother; and they deny that Jehovah has ever had any truck
with either nymphs or goddesses.
—*Robert Graves,* King Jesus

Why bastard? wherefore base? When my dimensions are
as well compact, my mind as generous and my shape as
true, as honest madam's issue? Why brand they us with
base? with baseness? bastardy? base, base?
—*William Shakespeare,* King Lear

Artificial insemination was the first method of noncoital conception
(that is, without sexual intercourse) to be developed. It involves a
simple technique of injecting sperm obtained through masturbation
into the vagina and can even be performed at home with a pharmacy
syringe (or turkey baster). Its most common application today is in
the alleviation of male infertility with the use of donor sperm. Typically, a married man consents to his wife's impregnation with sperm
from an anonymous stranger and assumes full paternal responsibility
for the child that is born. In normative terms this implies the separation of male biological and social parenting functions in a deviation from traditional norms of sexual reproduction within marriage.
Indeed, the ultimate legal response to issues raised by this method
of alternative reproduction was to reject the applicability of the
norms of adultery and illegitimacy and to develop in their place a
kind of contract model giving binding effect to the primary intentions of the involved parties. But artificial insemination was a widespread medical procedure long before legal change occurred. As part

of a general process of the medicalization of human reproduction, the professional ethics of the practice were informed by an attitude that scientized and objectified the notion of motherhood as natural destiny. Most important, the sexual insinuations of the practice strongly affected the medical monopoly, resulting in a protectionist principle of secrecy and donor anonymity along the lines of closed adoption.

The first reported case of artificial insemination in human beings is attributed to an English surgeon, Dr. John Hunter, in 1799, not long after the invention of the microscope and the consequent identification of sperm, and following a 1765 report by a German scientist, Dr. L. Jacobi, of artificial fertilization of fish eggs, as well as a 1785 report by an Italian priest, Abbé Lazarro Spallanzani, who first experimented with this technique on mammals and achieved a pregnancy in a female dog. The Talmud contains a discussion (dating to the second century A.D.) as to whether the high priest may marry a pregnant virgin, and according to the Midrash, a certain Ben-Sirah was allegedly conceived noncoitally by his father, Jeremiah, and an unnamed sister, but the Talmudic discussion is supposed to be purely academic and the Midrash account a legend. Likewise, Arab sources dating to 1322 that mention the fertilization of mares with semen stolen from breeding stallions belonging to a hostile tribe and the insemination of mares belonging to an enemy clan with the semen of inferior stallions are generally regarded as legends.[1] And the most famous intimation of noncoital conception in ancient literature—the New Testament account, in Luke 1:27–35, of the immaculate conception of Jesus—is certainly considered to lack scientific grounds.

In 1866 a leading American gynecologist, Dr. Marion Sims, reported fifty-five artificial inseminations performed on six women with one successful pregnancy. He later recanted his championing of the procedure, proclaiming it immoral. But Sims's publication gave the impetus to further experimentation and publications, mainly in Europe, and by 1934, 127 cases with 52 achieved pregnancies had been reported. All involved inseminating a woman with her husband's sperm on the thesis that introduction of semen directly to the cervix facilitates conception.[2] Three reports of donor insemination, published by two American physicians in 1903 and 1909, evoked a storm of public indignation against the sinful and adulterous character of the procedure.[3] A survey of 1941 based on questionnaires sent to 30,000 physicians in the United States and 7,642 responses, however, revealed that 9,489 women had conceived at least once through artificial insemination and that donor sperm had been used to achieve 3,649 pregnancies. In 1,357 cases more than one pregnancy had been effected by this means.[4] The gathering of statistical data on the dimensions of the practice was and still is impeded by the policy of maintaining secrecy. But by 1957 it was estimated that the number of children born in the United States from donor insemination alone exceeded 100,000. In 1960 one authority placed the estimate of donor insemination births at between 5,000 and 7,000 each year. The most recent estimate, in 1979, is that between 6,000 and 10,000 children are born annually by means of donor insemination in the United States.[5]

Reproduction without Sex

The first book on artificial insemination, by one Rohleder,[6] was published in 1934, one year before Aldous Huxley's *Brave New World*. By contemporary standards discourse on reproduction had clear sexual connotations (much as the emergence of the medical practice of obstetrics and gynecology in the nineteenth century was feared to have unavoidable sexual implications due to the intimacy of the male doctor and female patient, and the distribution of birth control literature was prohibited under the 1873 Comstock obscenity laws[7]). The inside cover of Rohleder's book listed a selection of publications by the same press, under the titles Bestiality ("the sexual connections include almost every animal, from goats to gorillas and from cats to crocodiles"), Madame Sex ("gruesome perversions rub shoulders with normal love"), and The Gods of Generation ("the most comprehensive guide on the worship of obscene Gods and phallic religions"). Indeed, in places the author's supposedly scientific treatment of the subject smacked of lewd sensationalism.

In any event, contemporary attitudes are well reflected in the book. To inseminate a woman with sperm from a man other than her husband was considered "just as much of a sin as if she had herself consorted with a strange man." Donor insemination was to be performed "only in desperate, exceptional cases, and to avoid a great disaster," such as where "the man is convinced of his incapacity and realises that he will have to leave all his fortune, the fruit of a lifetime of activity to strangers, or to adopt someone else's child," or where "the sterility had engendered grave psychic disturbances and dangerous depressive states which threatened to become severe and incurable psychoses, or to eventuate in suicide or at least divorce."[8] The passage is vague as to whether the victim of these psychic disturbances is the male or female spouse. Indeed, even though donor insemination is a solution to male infertility, throughout Rohleder's book it is referred to as a therapeutic device to eliminate sterility in a woman and fulfill her longing for a child. ("For after all, not every young girl is so hyper-modern as to enter marriage with the thought of never becoming a mother."[9]) Although it was already known that a childless marriage could be attributed to the male partner, the blame for childlessness was normally ascribed to the woman. Any suggestion of male blame aroused serious anxieties because of the cultural association of sterility with lack of masculinity. Hence, the woman was labeled as "sterile" and considered "the patient."[10]

At the same time, all arrangements regarding the procedure were made with the husband alone so as "to save the modesty of the woman." Since female orgasm was considered an important factor in the physiological process of conception, Rohleder recommended that insemination be performed "while the woman is in the stage of sexual excitement." In the case of insemination with the husband's sperm, the procedure was performed immediately after intercourse in private by the husband and wife, with a condom (to retain the sperm), after which the physician would enter and introduce the sperm in the husband's presence and with his assistance. In the case of donor insemination, Rohleder recommended that the husband "titillate the genitalia of his wife" to attain the state of sexual excitement conducive to conception. Although these procedures violated the woman's modesty, her passionate desire to become a mother would enable her to overcome her shame and to endure the continuing ordeal of infertility therapy. After insemination the woman's knees were tied together with a towel, and she was directed to remain in bed and avoid all movement for several hours and to refrain from such physical activities as riding and dancing for several weeks.[11]

The emphasis on the need for the woman's sexual excitement was probably a projection of the male reproductive experience that ejaculation of sperm involves orgastic pleasure.[12] But it also reflects the intellectual and moral difficulty of separating reproductive from sexual activity and illustrates well the intrusion of modern medicine into the marital relation. A certain skepticism about the effectiveness of the novel procedure raised serious concern that the wife was in fact committing adultery with a strange man, perhaps the administering physician himself, under the pretext of artificial insemination. Although insemination with the husband's sperm soon gained professional respectability and ceased to be regarded as posing any serious legal, social, or moral complications, donor insemination continued to be problematic, and the medical professional needed protection against the suggestion that he facilitated or participated in adulterous acts. In one case donor insemination was performed successfully, but the husband then began to drink heavily and accused his wife of infidelity with the physician. Three months later the husband apologized to the doctor, but after the child's birth, when the couple were taking leave of the doctor at the maternity clinic, a nurse said by way of a joke that the baby looked like the doctor. The husband apparently went out to get a taxi, and when he returned he drew out a revolver, fired at his wife and the baby, neither of whom was injured, and then shot himself dead.[13]

Secrecy and Anonymity

Because of the insinuation of adultery, there evolved a strict policy of secrecy and donor anonymity, reminiscent of the model of closed adoption and rationalized on similar grounds. Anonymity would prevent the wife from transferring her affection from her husband to the father of her child. (Indeed, *alienation of affections* is a technical term for *adultery* in torts law.) But instances of so-called moral jeopardy were rare. According to one story, a woman who failed to conceive through artificial insemination with sperm of her husband's friend, subsequently followed the advice of her husband to have sexual intercourse with the friend and became pregnant. Another woman supposedly stole her clinical records, which listed the donor's name, tracked him down, and left her husband to marry him. The fear that the wife would become attached to the donor probably stemmed from the conception that women had an overwhelming maternal urge of such libidinal force as to outweigh any emotional relation toward marital partners; this is a recurring theme in the early literature.[14] More recent works, though, tended to show that, far from being disruptive to the marital relation, the birth of a donor insemination child actually strengthened the emotional ties of the spouses.[15]

Although it appears that the initial practice of donor insemination was for the husband to choose a sperm donor (usually a relative), the physician later claimed the prerogative to select a donor, it being considered critical that the couple and donor be unacquainted.[16] According to the 1979 Curie-Cohen survey of the practice of donor insemination in the United States, 91.8 percent of the practitioners never allowed the recipient to select a donor, and the rest only rarely.[17]

Donor anonymity would also protect those involved, as in closed adoption. The donor would be protected from any claims by the child to support or inheritance rights. And the childless couple would be protected against blackmail by a donor who might threaten to divulge the controversial method of conception. Anonymity would also prevent the possibility of the sperm donor appearing suddenly on the scene and intruding into the family, which would disrupt the child's emotional well-being, in light of the child's ignorance of how he or she was conceived.[18]

Of course, if the matter were open in the first place, grounds for concern about possible blackmail by the donor would not exist. Similarly, if the child were apprised about the circumstances of her or his conception, the presence of the donor might be explained without any disastrous effect on the child's emotional well-being. Moreover, the family protection rationale was inconsistent with the donor protection rationale—if the donor's main concern was to protect himself from legal responsibility for the child, what would induce him to reveal his identity by intruding into the family environment?

But secrecy was also a practical means to avoid confrontation of various legal issues. Determination of parent-child relations in the law rested on the assumption that reproduction occurred as a result of sexual intercourse, and legal relations were a direct consequence of biological relation unless established through formal adoption procedures. In donor insemination the intention of all parties was to dissociate the donor's biological and legal connection to the child, but it was not at all clear that these intentions would be acknowledged and effectuated by the legal system. The uncertainty over the donor's legal responsibility toward the child was seen as discouraging men from offering their services for this purpose. Formal adoption by the infertile husband could have resolved the legal uncertainty but would have meant giving up the secrecy that was considered a self-evident necessity.[19]

Secrecy also allowed for the pretense of a normal pregnancy within marriage, thus avoiding exposure of the sensitive and shameful subject of the husband's infertility.[20] For this reason physicians would usually attempt to match the donor's physical characteristics (height, coloring, blood type) to those of the husband. Some physicians advocated the use of mixed sperm (that is, a combination of sperm from various donors and from the infertile husband), which made it impossible to identify the biological father if pregnancy ensued and had the advantage of at least creating an illusion of the possibility of the husband's paternity. Others inseminated the woman with separate sperm from two or more donors within any one cycle. Professional opinion was divided as to whether it was desirable to maintain records of the procedure. When it came time to name the father on the child's birth certificate, most physicians intentionally falsified the records, while others preferred to refer the woman to another obstetrician who did not know how she had conceived and could register the husband as the child's father in ignorant good faith. Above all, the child was never, under any circumstances, to be told the truth about his or her origins.[21]

In general, donor insemination was seen to have various advantages over adoption as a solution to childlessness: the genetic relation of the child to the wife, the experience of pregnancy as preparation for parenthood, satisfaction of the maternal urge, and the relative unlimited availability of prospective children. But a principle advantage was the pretense of marital reproduction and the ease with which the true circumstances of conception could be concealed. The question of the significance of biological heritage to the child's self-identity was considered a virtual nonissue so long as secrecy was maintained.[22] Due to this policy, and the consequent difficulty of identifying donor insemination families, virtually no research data are available on the emotional effect of donor anonymity on the child.

Medicalized Conception

The physician's professional interest in protecting his reputation made it only natural that he assert as much control as possible over the entire procedure. The greater the control, the less the chance that the secret practice would leak out and that he would be judged unethical for condoning acts performed by other persons involved in the procedure or held responsible for the consequences. The resultant process of medicalization extended the hold of the male-dominated practice of obstetrics and gynecology (to the exclusion of female traditional midwivery) while setting patterns for the later developments of surrogacy and in vitro fertilization that were influenced by patriarchal notions of women and motherhood as much as by professional self-interest. At the same time we see the establishment of a code of professional conduct that was eventually enacted into law through legislation.

Since medical training is not really necessary to perform the relatively simple procedure of artificial insemination and no elaborate instruments are required, some medical professionals were concerned that the practice would fall into the hands of so-called charlatans or quacks. In fact, however, the examples of nonmedical administration brought in the early literature related to "self-insemination" and involved no unlicensed third party. The most famous report was the "candle case" of 1905 in Coblenz, Germany. After six years of marriage a child had been born although the husband was impotent and no sexual intercourse had taken place during the relevant period. The husband claimed that the child was the illegitimate consequence of his wife's adultery, but she convinced the court that she had conceived after introducing "seminal fluid derived from a nocturnal pollution in bed" with the help of a candle.[23] In another case, a female prison inmate became pregnant, even though she had had no contact with men except for brief monthly meetings with her fiancé in the presence of a prison guard. It transpired that the fiancé had given the inmate a vial containing his sperm during one of these visits and that she had taken a syringe from the prison doctor's office, where she worked as an assistant, and introduced the sperm into her vagina by herself.[24]

It appears that physicians originally encouraged self-insemination in cases of artificial insemination with the husband's sperm as a convenient solution to the embarrassment of the physician's intrusion into the couple's intimacy. But later this convenience was considered insufficient to justify the loss of professional control. Indeed, physicians who left administration of the procedure to midwives and nurses were regarded as abetting a malpractice analogous to quackery in abortion.[25] In addition to actual administration of the procedure, professional control was asserted with respect to determining patient eligibility, selecting donors, and keeping records.

Physicians determined patient eligibility according to criteria similar to those applied by adoption agencies, with particular attention to the psychology of the childless woman. Generally, artificial insemination would be performed only if the woman was married and her husband had consented. The couple were subjected to an investigation to satisfy the physician that artificial insemination was not being used "as a mortar to cement a shaky union" and that the child would enjoy an emotionally stable and economically comfortable family environment. The wife's response to the condition of childlessness was crucial because of the common perception that a woman's "full psychic role" hinged on motherhood, whereas a man's reproductive propensity was secondary to other spheres of social activity. The ideal female candidate was the "truly motherly woman" who responded to childlessness by transferring her maternal sentiments to other people, specifically her husband. The woman who refused to accept her husband's infertility passively and actively desired a child of her own was labeled "masculine aggressive." Opponents of donor insemination even argued that the true human love of a woman expressed itself in wanting her husband's child, whereas the desire for "just a child" was a mere animal urge.[26]

The ineligibility of unmarried women was explained in terms of the sex roles of the patriarchal two-parent family. Economic factors might force an unmarried woman to go out to work, supposedly leaving the child without any care. Even if she were financially independent the lack of a father figure would be detrimental to the child and would also jeopardize the mother's secrecy. The very motivation of an unmarried woman to conceive through artificial insemination was considered pathological, demonstrating "ruthless selfishness." Women of this kind were "too independent, too domineering to submit to matrimony . . . taking up a defiant attitude towards the male sex, implying that they had no need to beg favours of the lords of creation."[27] Even as late as 1976 we find the opinion that "any display of interest in this operation by an unmarried woman is indicative of psychological distress."[28] But professional norms have changed somewhat in this respect, and 10 percent of the respondents to the Curie-Cohen survey of 1979 cited the unmarried state of the woman as an indication for donor insemination.[29]

Medical control over the selection of sperm donors was indicated by the eugenic aspects of the procedure as much as by a concern for confidentiality. The common belief was that the risk of a malpractice suit existed primarily in relation to a poor choice of donor, and careful selection was regarded as the physician's exclusive and cardinal responsibility.[30] The potential of artificial insemination techniques in the breeding of superior species was much appreciated and applied in the field of animal husbandry. Although human eugenics fell into moral disrepute in the wake of the experiments conducted under the Nazi regime, professional criteria for donor selection continued to carry a eugenic undertone. Thus the physician who formulated what came to be the generally accepted criteria suggested that "the physician should be guided by animal husbandrymen who select superior sires and prize stallions almost entirely by their physical fitness . . . it [being] just as necessary to investigate the family lineage of a human donor as it is for the workers of stud farms to select prize males based on ancestry in order to obtain a better grade of offspring."[31]

The original practice was to use married men with at least two healthy children as a guarantee of the donor's fertility and the quality of his progeny. The disadvantage of married donors was that the wife's consent was required as a matter of ethics, which meant involving another person in the secret procedure. In spite of the later development of laboratory analysis of semen, 96 percent of respondents to the Curie-Cohen survey of 1979 required nothing more than a routine family medical history from the donor.[32] Genetic screening, if at all performed, was limited to identifying certain ethnic hereditary diseases, such as sickle-cell anemia, Tay-Sachs disease, and most recently AIDS (acquired immunodeficiency syndrome). One reason for this laxity in screening is that donors were, and still are, largely recruited from the male student population in medical schools. Candidates for the profession were supposed to have the character, intellect, and cooperative personality necessary to a confidential practice in which the need for sperm is determined by the rhythm of the physican's practice and the woman's ovulatory cycle.[33]

The first sperm donors were apparently practitioners' colleagues, on whom they could rely to keep the procedure secret, and it is not inconceivable that physicians used their own sperm in donor insemination. In selecting what they considered "superior" genes for donor insemination, the practitioners thus chose to reproduce themselves. According to one early report, a donor who was "an eminent figure in his profession," a married man with two children, had "sired" thirteen donor insemination children.[34] In these circumstances anonymity was also a measure of protection against injury to the donor's professional reputation.

In 1947 a group of enterprising medical students in New York City offered confidential service in supplying sperm from "healthy and investigated professional donors." Apparently this notice gave rise to fear about the possible spread of venereal disease, as well as to general concern about the operation of a commercial enterprise not subject to norms of professional conduct. The Department of Health subsequently issued a regulation that permitted the sale of human semen for artificial insemination only by a licensed physician.[35]

Within a few years professionally supervised sperm banks emerged, employing newly developed scientific techniques for sperm analysis and preservation in frozen storage. But the Curie-Cohen survey revealed that only 15 percent of practitioners used these services. In part this reflects a preference for fresh, as opposed to frozen, sperm, but more generally the use of a sperm bank means loss of control for the individual practitioner over donor selection and record keeping. This would be problematic, for example, if a donor insemination couple returned to their physician and requested a second child from the same donor.[36] What is more, the sperm bank poses a real threat of male redundancy in reproduction, which is good enough reason—albeit unconscious—for a male-dominated profession to retain control.

Record keeping also raised problems of secrecy. Although the husband's written consent might prevent future disputes, it would have little value as a defense against criminal charges of adultery. At least one prominent practitioner considered that sound screening of the couple rendered all documentation superfluous.[37] As practitioners grew confident in their screening methods they not only ceased to require documentary proof of the husband's consent but even advised the couple, for the sake of secrecy, not to keep any personal papers relating to the procedure.[38]

More important, perhaps, was the general failure to keep records of the sperm donors as part of the imperative of anonymity. According to the Curie-Cohen survey, 93 percent of the practitioners kept records of the recipient couples, 37 percent of the children (though as many as 50 percent provided obstetric care for the pregnant inseminated woman), and only 30 percent of the donors. Of the respondents, 83 percent opposed a suggestion to legislate mandatory record keeping on grounds of the principle of anonymity.[39] Lack of genetic information has obvious implications for the resulting child's medical history, and the psychological importance of biological self-knowledge has already been noted above in the context of closed adoption.

Playing God

Practitioners wielded immense authority in determining norms of professional conduct. Candidates for artificial insemination could be expected to comply with almost any requirement their physician posited, as is still the case today with infertility therapy. The moral insinuation of adultery that underlay the professional policy of secrecy, for example, might not have concerned the lay patients to the same extent. A 1951 survey of over three hundred Norwegian childless couples showed that 77 percent of the respondents did not regard the procedure as either adulterous or immoral, and 62 percent said they would undergo it even if required by law to apply to a public committee.[40] Likewise, sensitivity about male infertility might not have been as significant as doctors perceived. In 1954 two artificial insemination practitioners in the United States sent a questionnaire to thirty-eight recipient couples, asking each spouse separately about his or her reasons for choosing donor insemination over adoption. The replies were as follows: closer relationship to infant, 62 percent (32 men, 15 women); dissatisfaction with adoption procedures, 61 percent (25 men, 21 women); maternal heredity, 55 percent (22 men, 20 women); desire to experience pregnancy, 51 percent (16 men, 23 women). Only 18 percent (6 men, 8 women) mentioned the concealment of infertility.[41]

The policy of secrecy seems in general to have exceeded the bounds of necessity and crossed the gray area that marks the boundary between confidentiality and deceptive falsification. As Britain's Warnock Committee pointed out in 1984 in its report on human fertilization techniques, the sense that a secret exists may undermine the whole network of family relationships. "AID [Artificial Insemination–Donor] children may feel obscurely that they are being deceived by their parents, that they are in some way different from their peers, and that the men whom they regard as their fathers are not their real fathers."[42] In addition, the attempt to avoid invading the physical intimacy of the marital relation through the physician's mediation between the sperm donor and the childless couple resulted in the depersonalization of social relations of reproduction. The physician not only arrogated authority to make matches of reproductive collaboration—decisions normally made on a very personal basis— but also absolved the sperm donor from all practical responsibility for the consequences of his reproductive act. Anonymity may have avoided certain legal problems as to the donor's relation to the child, but it left much to be desired as a norm of male responsibility. A dissenting statement to Australia's Waller Report thus criticized "the clandestine manner in which the operation is performed and any record of the donor's identity concealed or destroyed, the possible incestuous union between parties related to or through the donor, the arbitrariness of allowing a doctor or laboratory assistant to decide who shall sire a woman's child, the immorality of paying donors for fathering children they will never know or care for as their own natural off-spring, and above all the debasement of human generation to stud-farming methods."[43]

The morality of selling sperm was not seriously questioned until the surrogacy debate framed it as a matter of gender equality, making it appear that a man was being paid to father children he would never know. The going fees for sperm "vendors" apparently range from twenty to as much as one hundred dollars per ejaculate. Experience with blood banks has shown that a paid donation service is medically and economically inferior to a voluntary system, since the finanical incentive encourages indigents to conceal relevant facts in medical history and so pollutes blood supply.[44] It seems, though, that the selection of sperm donors from among medical students, who are supposedly aware of the importance of disclosing medical history, was regarded as adequate protection against such dangers in the context of artificial insemination. Nevertheless, both Britain's Warnock Committee and Australia's Waller Committee recommended to prohibit fees for sperm donors beyond actually incurred expenses. The

Warnock Committee suggested that the French system of donor recruitment be adopted, according to which prospective donor insemination recipients are asked to approach their friends to make a voluntary donation to a sperm bank, not for the use of any particular recipient, much as patients requiring blood transfusion for surgery will ask family members or acquaintances to donate the required amount to the hospital's blood bank.[45]

Anonymous Donors and Reproductive Responsibility

Questions as to the sperm donor's responsibility arise beyond the issue of his remuneration. The donor who fathered thirteen children has been mentioned. Another report claimed the impregnation of thirty-five women with sperm from a single source.[46] The Curie-Cohen survey showed that 51 percent of responding practitioners averaged one or two pregnancies per donor, but 10 percent averaged nine or more, with one report of fifty pregnancies. Practitioners seemed more concerned with pragmatic considerations, but where policy was taken into account the norm was not more than six pregnancies.[47]

Although the principle of donor anonymity precluded substantial research on the attitudes of sperm donors, "the available information suggests that most donors have no thoughts about their action . . . 'it's the same as giving blood' is a common response."[48] One physician who called on his donors about once a week found that "most students are matter-of-fact about supplying spermatozoa; they recieve their fee on an impersonal basis and rarely ask leading questions or display any interest in the procedure after they hand over the receptacle."[49] According to yet another source, sperm donation was seen "as impersonal as transfusion from a blood bank and the relation between the recipient and the donor . . . just as intimate."[50]

The moral character of such "professional sperm vendors" has indeed been criticized, primarily by Catholic theologians. The act of sperm donation motivated solely by financial gain, according to this view, is tantamount to prostitution, and the physician is thus akin to a common pimp. The procedure supposedly involves a humanitarian act of masturbation, but in effect it amounts to human stud-farming with men behaving like breeding animals.[51]

This is one writer's response to a claim that the physician exercised such high criteria regarding the donor's personality as would satisfy the writer's own standards for a son-in-law: "I would not want [my daughter] to marry a man whose realization of the responsibilities of parenthood was so slight that he would be willing to father a child, or many children, whom he would never see and towards whom he would have no duty, and this, moreover through a woman he does not even know."[52] In this view the moral difficulty with the donor's act is that "a man should take full responsibility for the off-spring of his loins—a moral obligation not invalidated by acquiescence in the irresponsibility of fathers towards their bastard sons." The donor's obligation is not met by the assurance that "someone" will be responsible for his child. "The responsibility is exclusively *his,* because of the moral relationship assumed to derive from, and to attend, paternity; to beget without the possibility of a continuing father-child relationship, would be to withdraw biological potential from personal potential. . . . In a defined sense, therefore, the donor's action, made possible by human science, is anti-human: it isolates biological potential from the human potential."[53]

The identification of biological fatherhood with continuing social responsibility for the child as a matter of unshakable moral obligation stems from a religious deontological approach to the "natural law" of reproduction. A secular teleological approach takes into account the purposes and consequences of an act in passing value judgment on its propriety. Human responsibilities need not be conclusively and specifically determined by biological capacities. Degrees of moral accountability for the exercise of one's reproductive capacity can vary between the two extremes of isolation and identification of biological and human potentials.

The question is, therefore, *what* social responsibilities toward the child attach to genetic parenthood. The Catholic view is: all those responsibilities that attach in the case of marital reproduction—that is, for all the material and spiritual needs of the child. A counterview, espoused in support of the current norm of donor anonymity, is that the donor's moral obligations regarding the use of his genetic material are satisfied by the knowledge that the child will be born into a relationship that contains a surrogate social father and that such knowledge distinguishes the sperm donor from the "sailor with a girl in every port who goes around the world irresponsibly scattering his Maker's image."[54]

The donor himself has no control over his sperm once it has been ejaculated and therefore cannot know anything about the social circumstances of his offspring. But the medical practitioner can be assumed to have such knowledge. Indeed, current professional ethical norms appear adequate in this respect. Although the potential for abuse present in the discretionary intervention of a detached party in matters of reproduction must always be borne in mind, no manifestation of such abuse appears in present medical practices. Likewise, even if we assume that a child's genetic origin as such is of little, if any, consequence as regards his or her social relations and welfare (although a thorough inquiry into the relation between genetic identity and self-identity requires full disclosure of the relevant information), this does not resolve the question of the significance of a person's genetic materials for himself.

In this respect the sperm donor and the virile sailor appear to share a similarity. The donor relinquishes his parental obligation through the quasi-adoption service of a mediating physician, who undertakes to "place" the sperm with a parent who remains unknown to the donor but whose parental fitness is assured by the physician; the sailor leaves a child with a woman who probably appreciated the risk of pregnancy when she agreed to consort with him and knew that he would be unavailable to assist in raising the child. In both cases others implicitly consent to the man's abrogation of parental responsibility, but that is not to say that he has acted responsibly.

The sailor is irresponsible in that he probably did not concern himself significantly with a potential pregnancy, and if he did, he likely considered it the woman's responsibility, manifesting the traditional sexual-reproductive double standard. The woman's implicit acceptance of parental responsibility is not a morally valid exemption of the man from responsibility, since she too labors under the same cultural double standard. The sailor's conduct is morally reprehensible chiefly regarding the woman on whom he, by default, places all responsibility for a child who, one may assume, neither party intended to come into being.

The donor, by contrast, is assumed to act with the intention of effecting a pregnancy in a woman who has freely chosen to assume social responsibility for the consequences of conception. His conduct thus cannot be faulted as regards his responsibility to the woman. Rather, the donor's irresponsibility relates to the frame of mind within which he provides his sperm—that is, to the integrity of his intentional act. He can be regarded as acting responsibly only to the extent that he has fully appreciated the meaning of his act. This is primarily a matter of accountability toward oneself.

The anonymous donor functions as the mechanical producer of an off-white liquid substance that contains genetic material. A sperm bank administrator or physician pays him his dues and thereafter owns the liquid and disposes of it as he or she deems fit. In this detached and impersonal manner the donor dissociates his material function from its concrete human consequence—the creation of a new life. He implicitly denies that his sperm contains the seed of a future human being. Even if his procreative act does not in itself define the scope of his responsibility toward the resulting child, it has a significance that is wholly suppressed by the emotional alienation that accompanies the donor's physical separation from his sperm. The donor may or may not wish to assume personal responsibility for the ongoing nurture of the child, but his reproductive activity is more than a matter of excreting a bodily substance.[55] Interestingly, legislation passed recently in Sweden to allow artificial insemination children access to information about their biological fathers on reaching the age of maturity resulted in a significant drop in the number of men willing to act as sperm donors.[56]

Artificial Insemination and the Law

The principle of donor anonymity reinforces the norm of male reproductive irresponsibility. Women, obviously, are far more involved emotionally in the reproductive process, and if a claim for equal treatment of sperm donor and surrogate mother is made, by no means is the intention for women to imitate men's behavioral irresponsibility. On the contrary, the female's connection with her offspring provides a model for criticizing men's alienation.

At the same time the issue of gender equality arises when one looks at how the law defines the parent-child relation. In artificial insemination with a donor the tacit agreement is that the biological father will not be held responsible as the legal father for the child. In surrogacy there is a similar agreement that the biological mother relinquishes her legal relation to the child. At the same time the social relation between the child and the sponsoring parents—the biological mother and her husband in artificial insemination, and the biological father and his wife in surrogacy—calls for legal definition.

Within traditional legal rubrics the artificial insemination child was illegitimate, being born to a married woman but not from her husband. Under common law the child could be legitimated through the subsequent marriage of her biological parents, but this was obviously incompatible with the whole purpose of artificial insemination, which was to fertilize an existing childless marriage. The basic common law rule was ameliorated by a legal presumption that evolved in nineteenth-century court decisions according to which any child born in the duration of a marriage was regarded as the legitimate offspring of the husband-wife union. The presumption would be rebutted, however, if paternity was disproved through evidence of blood tests or of the artificial insemination procedure itself.[57]

Issues of the artificial insemination child's legal status were generally avoided by the child's de facto incorporation into what appeared to be a natural family. But when such issues did arise in several cases of marital breakdown, the general approach of the courts was to avoid branding the child as illegitimate. The ultimate resolution of the donor insemination family's legal status by the judiciary, and subsequently by the legislature, can be explained in terms of an implicit rationale that the social relations of the reproducing adults and their prior-to-conception intentions—rather than any biological connection—were the significant factors in establishing a legal father-child relation. This was an innovation also in relation to the law of adoption, which does not challenge the initial establishment of the parent-child relation on grounds of biology but merely divests and transfers it from the biological parent to another after the child's birth.

Judicial Response

The first donor artificial insemination case in the United States, *Hoch v. Hoch* (1945), was an action for divorce on grounds of the wife's adultery, the husband having returned from military service to find his wife with child.[58] The wife's defense against the charge of adultery was that the child had been conceived through artificial insemination with donor sperm. The facts were, to say the least, unfavorable to the legal debut of artificial insemination: the couple's physical separation and the husband's ignorance of the procedure were sufficient to cast suspicion on the truth of the wife's contention.[59] The attempt to explain a clearly extramarital pregnancy as resulting from a new method of noncoital conception must have justified the concern that it posed an unavoidable threat to the institution of marriage. But, although it rejected the defense of donor artificial insemination on the facts, the court opined that had it been proved it would *not* have constituted adultery.

This issue was litigated directly in one other case, and decided contrarily. In *Doornbos v. Doornbos* (1954), the wife filed a complaint for divorce, seeking custody of her child, and argued that the husband had no claim in such respect since the child had been born as a result of donor artificial insemination.[60] The husband responded by claiming visitation rights on grounds of the presumption that he was the father of a child born within the marriage, without either denying or conceding that the child had been conceived through donor artificial insemination. At the same time he asked the court to order disclosure of the inseminating physician's name in order to interrogate him as to his part in "this alliance and conspiracy" and to punish him if his conduct were found to be "unlawful and against

moral and natural laws." The court held that donor artificial insemination constituted adultery with or without the husband's consent,
that the child was therefore illegitimate, and that the husband had no
legal rights in relation to the child.[61]

The question of adultery was finally addressed by the Supreme
Court of California in what came to be considered a comprehensive
landmark judicial pronouncement on the legality of donor artificial
insemination. *People v. Sorenson* (1968) was an appeal against the
husband's criminal conviction for failure to support a donor artificial
insemination child.[62] Since the husband had consented to the procedure, the court held *obiter dictum*[63] that the child was the lawful
offspring of the marriage and not the product of an adulterous relationship. The court stated:

> Adultery is defined as "the voluntary sexual intercourse of a
> married person with a person other than the offender's husband
> or wife". . . . It has been suggested that the doctor and the wife
> commit adultery by the process of artificial insemination. . . .
> Since the doctor may be a woman, or the husband himself may
> administer the insemination by a syringe, this is patently ab-
> surd; to consider it an act of adultery with the donor, who at the
> time of insemination may be a thousand miles away or may
> even be dead, is equally absurd.[64]

The definition of the legal relation between the husband and the
donor insemination child was of more immediate concern to the
courts than the issue of adultery. This question arose in connection
with child support and visitation and, in one instance, the husband's
right to veto the child's adoption by another man. In all these cases
conception through donor artificial insemination and the husband's
consent were factually established. The decisions were not of one
accord as regards classification of the child as illegitimate,[65] but with
the exception of the *Doornbos* case they all held that a legal relation
existed between husband and child.

If a child born of consensual donor artificial insemination was the
legitimate offspring of the marriage, the husband's parental relation
to the child would follow automatically. In *Strnad v. Strnad* (1948),
for instance, the court acknowledged the husband's visitation right,

stating briefly that the child had been "semiadopted" by him and that she was as legitimate as a child born out-of-wedlock who had been subsequently legitimated through her parents' marriage.[66] In *People v. Dennett* (1958) the court similarly refused to allow the wife to challenge her husband's right to visitation on grounds of his biological disrelation to the children. The spouses had entered a separation agreement referring to the children as the issue of the marriage, with which they both complied over a period of two years. The court interpreted the wife's conduct as recognizing the husband's parental relation and refused to stigmatize the children as bastards.[67] In *Gursky v. Gursky* (1963) the court annulled a marriage for lack of consummation despite the birth of a donor insemination child with the husband's consent. It considered the child illegitimate but held the husband to a duty of child support because his consent implied a promise to support any resulting offspring, and the wife presumably would not have undergone the procedure otherwise.[68]

The *Sorenson* court also relied on the intentions behind the actions that led to the child's conception in concluding that the husband was criminally liable for nonsupport of the child. Since the relevant provision in the criminal code applied expressly to "a father of either a legitimate or illegitimate minor child," the question of illegitimacy was immaterial, and the question facing the court was whether the husband should be defined as "a father." It answered:

> Under the facts of this case, the term "father" . . . cannot be limited to the biologic or natural father as those terms are generally understood. The determinative factor is whether the legal relationship of father and child exists. A child conceived through heterologous [that is, donor] artificial insemination does not have a "natural father", as that term is commonly used. The anonymous donor of the sperm cannot be considered the "natural father", as he is no more responsible for the use made of his sperm than is the donor of blood or a kidney. Since there is no "natural father", we can only look for a lawful father.[69]

Having thus asserted a distinction between the biological and legal father, the court concluded that the consenting husband was indeed the donor insemination child's legal father:

A reasonable man who, because of his inability to procreate, actively participates and consents to his wife's artificial insemination in the hope that a child will be produced whom they will treat as their own, knows that such behavior carries with it the legal responsibilities of fatherhood and criminal responsibility for nonsupport. One who consents to the production of a child cannot create a temporary relation to be assumed and disclaimed at will, but the arrangement must be of such character as to impose an obligation of supporting those for whose existence he is directly responsible.[70]

In re Adoption of Anonymous (1973) drew on the same reasoning to hold that the husband was a "parent" for the purpose of an adoption statute requiring parental consent. There the wife had remarried after divorce and her new husband wished to adopt the artificial insemination child. The first husband had consistently exercised visitation rights and fulfilled support obligations in accord with a divorce decree that referred to the child as the couple's "daughter" and "child." The 1963 *Gursky* case, decided in the same jurisdiction, had held the artificial insemination child to be illegitimate, and if so the father's consent to adoption would not be required. But the court dismissed that holding as unpersuasive, because it was clear that the traditional norm of illegitimacy had not contemplated the practice of artificial insemination and it would serve no purpose to stigmatize the child or to compel the parents formally to adopt in order to confer on her the status of a naturally conceived child. The court stated further: "An AID child is not 'begotten' by a father who is not the husband; the donor is anonymous; the wife does not have sexual intercourse or commit adultery with him; if there is any 'begetting' it is by the doctor who in this specialty is often a woman."[71]

Indeed, in terms of factual causation the donor and physician (whether male or female) are as responsible for the child's "begetting" and existence as the husband and wife. The different normative significance that attaches to the conduct of the various participants in the insemination procedure can be explained only by reference to the intentions and expectations that accompany their actions. That is, the husband is responsible for the child as a legal parent because the entire procedure is informed by the understanding that he intends to raise the child with his wife as their own and that the donor and physician will be absolved from any such responsibility.

Legislative Response

The *Strnad* case of 1948 had pierced the veil of secrecy that allowed the public and their political representatives to ignore the challenge of the donor artificial insemination procedure to traditional norms of reproduction. Two subsequent bills introduced in the New York Senate failed to pass, the opposition apparently stemming from the view that the rights of the parties were obvious and legislation unnecessary.[72] Moral controversy clearly played a role in delaying legislation, however. The sponsor of a Minnesota bill of 1949 reported that he and the members of his family had suffered personal abuse and received vicious anonymous phone calls and that some religious groups had become fanatic on the subject. Because the primary concern of the involved parties (physicians, donors, and childless couples) was to maintain secrecy, there was no active organized lobby for appropriate legislative action.[73]

By the mid-1960s, however, conflicting judicial rulings on the donor insemination child's status had produced a fair amount of confusion, reflecting the inadequacy of the traditional norms to deal with the new social conditions. In 1968 the National Law Commission included a section on artificial insemination in the Uniform Parentage Act, adopting a family relations approach equivalent to that of the *Sorenson* decision. Section 5 provided:

(a) If . . . with the consent of her husband, a wife is inseminated artificially with the semen donated by a man not her husband, the husband is treated in law as if he were the natural father of a child thereby conceived. . . .

(b) the donor of semen provided . . . for use in artificial insemination of a married woman other than the donor's wife is treated in law as if he were not the natural father of a child thereby conceived.

Approximately half the states now have some form of donor insemination legislation, the general thrust being to establish the legitimate paternal relation of the husband to a child born of consensual donor artificial insemination within the marriage and to negate all legal consequences from the fact of the sperm donor's biological paternity.[74] As mentioned, the implicit rationale of this scheme is that the social parent-child relation can be established independent of biology through autonomous consent: the donor's biological connection with the child is void of normative significance and the husband bears legal responsibility for the child—all in accord with the intent of the involved parties before conception.

The same reasoning threads through a series of recent cases that differed in various ways from the typical circumstances contemplated by *Sorenson* and the legislation on artificial insemination. In *C.M. v. C.C.* (1977), for example, an unmarried woman inseminated herself with sperm provided by a friend, who then claimed visitation rights with respect to the child.[75] The man testified that they had been dating and even contemplating marriage and that he had assumed he would act toward the child as a father, whereas the woman testified that the intention was different and that he was only to visit her home like other male friends. The court believed the man and held that he was the child's "natural father" and entitled as such to visitation rights, distinguishing him from the donor in ordinary circumstances of artificial insemination where the anonymity implies a waiver of parental rights. The court reasoned that in this case the man was as much the child's father as if the couple were married and had used the husband's sperm for artificial insemination or as if they had conceived the child out of wedlock by sexual intercourse.

Another case in the same jurisdiction, *K.S. v. G.S.* (1981), raised the question whether the husband was legally obliged to support a donor insemination child where his consent had not been given in writing.[77] The court established that the husband initially gave oral consent. He argued, however, that he had withdrawn it at some point after his wife miscarried a pregnancy that resulted from a successful insemination. The court held as a matter of law that consent, once given, is presumed effective at the time pregnancy occurs unless the husband establishes by clear evidence that he later revoked it. It declared the husband to be the lawful father of the child since he had not met that burden of proof. A similar result was reached in *R.S. v. R.S.* (1983), where the court held the husband responsible for child support on the basis of his unrevoked oral consent, despite a statutory requirement of written consent.[77]

As intimated in *C.M. v. C.C.*, if the parent-child relation is established according to prior-to-conception intentions, the actual method of conception appears to be immaterial. Indeed, in *L.M.S. v. S.L.S.* (1983), the court followed the *Sorenson* rationale to determine the legal parenthood of a husband who agreed to his wife conceiving through sexual intercourse with a "surrogate father" after having unsuccessfully attempted to adopt a child and having dismissed artificial insemination because of the expense.[78] The biological father never established any social relationship with the child (or the mother for that matter) and voluntarily terminated parental rights according to their agreement.

Yet the analogy to donor artificial insemination fails if there is no agreement before or at conception that transfers to the husband the rights and duties normally attaching to the biological father. In *Byers v. Byers* (1980), for example, the question was whether a man who knowingly married a woman then pregnant by another man could be held liable to support the child as its legal father.[79] The court distinguished the case at bar from donor artificial insemination, noting that the wife had conceived before she met her husband and that the biological father's legal responsibility for the child remained unaltered. Likewise, *In re Adoption of McFadyen* (1982) denied the husband paternal status for the purpose of consent to adoption on finding that no prior-to-conception agreement had been established.[80] There the man and woman were married at the time of conception, but the husband had previously undergone a vasectomy, which rebutted the presumption of paternity with regard to a child born within a marital relation. The couple had agreed that the wife have intercourse with other men to become pregnant and considered this arrangement analogous to donor artificial insemination, referring to it as "artificial insemination by means of a surrogate donor's penis." The court, however, refused to reverse the trial court's factual finding that the couple had not proven the existence of a prior-to-conception agreement.

One more case is pertinent in this respect. *State ex rel H. v. P.* (1982), in which a husband sought custody and visitation rights with respect to a child born within the marriage and the wife challenged his paternity.[81] The wife had been enrolled with her husband's consent in an artificial insemination program, but she alleged that she had eventually conceived the child while on a business trip through intercourse with a man she refused to name. A few months after the child's birth the couple separated, and the husband regularly visited the child and paid support. He claimed that his wife never told him that the child was not conceived by donor artificial insemination until after the birth. The court stated that under any objective analysis of the competing claims, the husband never retreated from his intention to care for the child as his daughter, and it refused to allow the wife to contest his paternity. An order directing the husband to submit to blood tests was reversed, since his claim to paternity was not based on biological connection to the child.

The law of donor artificial insemination thus posits the radical conception that a man may exercise autonomy as a moral agent in determining the normative consequences of his reproductive acts and that the legal definition of fatherhood is not necessarily a matter of biological predetermination but rather of rational human intention. The dissociation of biological from social fatherhood in donor artificial insemination departed from the fundamental traditional norm that the legal parent-child relation attaches initially and as a matter of course to the biological relation. The legal issues that arose with respect to the social relations of reproduction in this context illuminated the normative content of the hitherto unquestioned equation of biological and social parenthood, and pointed to a proposition widely accepted in other fields of science, to wit, that scientific (in this case, biological) facts do not have inherent normative significance beyond that attached to them through the moral agency of human beings.

The normative significance of the blood relation under traditional law was part of a patriarchal social order that aimed at overcoming the uncertainty of biological fatherhood. Social conditions today require reevaluation of the relation between biological and social roles in the bearing and rearing of children. Medical technology now provides relatively efficient methods of birth control and noncoital conception that first separate sex and reproduction and then allow the conceptual differentiation of biological and social elements in these activities. Scientific control of reproduction thus affords options and expands the range of human autonomy in choosing the terms of social reproductive relations between consenting adults.

Is it then the case that the notion of family relations based on biology is making way for more sophisticated ways of reproductive collaboration, beyond the patriarchal mold of male domination and female/child subjection? Does the appearance of an openly nonbiological family indicate a new phase in male-female and adult-child relations? Is there any reason why parent-child relations ought *not* to be established through voluntary agreements between adults as to the use of their reproductive capacities? The law of artificial insemination apparently answers that there is no reason to justify contractual disability with respect to male reproductive potential. However, when we turn to the question of female autonomy in reproduction— as posed by the practice of surrogate mother arrangements—many objections arise, exemplifying again the traditional double standard that is supposedly justified by woman's peculiar biology.

CHAPTER 5

Surrogate Mother Arrangements

*Fancy an artist with a change of standards as you'd have a
change of shirts or of dinner-plates. To do it—to do it and
make it divine—is the only thing he has to think about. "Is
it done or not?" is his only question. Not "Is it done as
well as a proper solicitude for my dear little family will
allow?" He has nothing to do with the relative—he has
only to do with the absolute; and a dear little family may
represent a dozen relatives.*
—Henry James, The Lesson of the Master

Surrogate mother arrangements are a phenomenon of the last decade, and several hundred children have been born in this way in the
United States. Surrogacy emerged about the same time as the first
successful in vitro fertilization birth, and it was probably affected by
the prevailing attitude surrounding reproductive medicine that infertility is no longer a fate to be passively accepted but a condition
correctable through human technology if adoption is infeasible. It is
also likely that the idea of a woman bearing a child outside marriage
for a strange couple, as the female counterpart of the sperm donor,
grew out of the liberalization of sexual mores in the 1970s, as well
as the feminist critique of the confining bonds of motherhood.

A woman's role in any surrogacy arrangement clearly departs radically from the traditional norm of marital reproduction. But because
no sexual intercourse is involved and since the courts had already
rejected the applicability of norms of adultery and illegitimacy in
donor artificial insemination cases, the frame for legal discussion of
surrogacy has been dominated by the adoption and artificial insemination statutes. Although a contractual theory has found some
expression, the tendency, as explained in the Introduction, is to dis-
miss surrogacy as conflicting with the public policy of adoption law

and to distinguish it from donor artificial insemination in terms of biological difference.

Surrogacy and Artificial Insemination

I have already indicated that surrogacy presents a mirror situation to that of artificial insemination of a married woman with donor sperm. The simplest case of surrogacy involves a married couple who are involuntarily childless due to the wife's infertility. Another woman—the surrogate mother—agrees (for monetary consideration) to be artificially inseminated with the husband's sperm, to bear and give birth to a child thus conceived, and thereafter to give up the child to be reared by the childless couple. From the viewpoint of the childless couple surrogacy is therefore analogous to donor artificial insemination. The same technique of noncoital conception is used to provide a solution to infertility and produce a child biologically related to at least one of the couple. In donor artificial insemination the cause of the couple's childlessness is found in the male partner, in surrogacy, in the female. In one case the answer is to find a fertile male who will act as biological father to a child wanted by the couple, in the other it is to find a fertile female.

Although surrogacy shares many features with artificial insemination, it raises new questions about the legality of the collaboration and the legal status of the child. Artificial insemination statutes employ gender-specific language that applies to the particular social context of male infertility. I have already quoted section 5 of the Uniform Parentage Act, which provides:

(a) If . . . with the consent of her husband, a wife is inseminated artificially with semen donated by a man not her husband, the husband is treated in law as if he were the natural father of a child thereby conceived. . . .
(b) The donor of semen provided . . . for use in artificial insemination of a married woman other than the donor's wife is

treated in law as if he were not the natural father of a child thereby conceived.

In the surrogacy context of female infertility the effect of these terms is patently at odds with the intentions of the parties to the arrangement.[1] If the surrogate mother is a married woman and her husband consented, the effect of section 5 would be to establish the legal parenthood of the surrogate and her husband, on the one hand, and to void the biological relation between the commissioning husband ("the donor of semen") and the child of any legal consequences, on the other.

To avoid this it was necessary to have the surrogate's husband declare formally his *non*-consent to the artificial insemination procedure. In addition, the practice was to establish the commissioning couple's legal parenthood through a paternity action (with respect to the husband) and then a private adoption procedure (by the wife) after termination of the surrogate's parental rights. The paternity statutes also pose certain problems, however. In *Syrkowski v. Appleyard* (1985), for example, Mr. Syrkowski, a childless married man, entered into a monetary surrogacy agreement with Mrs. Appleyard, a married woman with two children. Mrs. Appleyard was artificially inseminated with Mr. Syrkowski's sperm in March 1981.[2] In June he filed a complaint under the Michigan Paternity Act requesting a determination that he was the legal father of the child, that his name be entered as father on the birth certificate, that the child bear his surname, and that he be awarded full custody of the child. In July the parties jointly filed for approval of a consent order of filiation, but in November Michigan's attorney general intervened in the proceedings, arguing, among other things, that the surrogate mother arrangement fell outside the scope of the Paternity Act, that the "semen donor" had no legal relationship to the child, and that Mr. Appleyard must be deemed the father of his wife's child both under the Michigan artificial insemination statute and because of a general statutory presumption as to the legitimacy of a child born in the course of a marriage. In response, Mr. Syrkowski filed a statement of nonconsent made by Mr. Appleyard in April 1981, which read as follows:

> I . . . acknowledge the existence of [the artificial insemination statute] . . . which provides, "A child born to a married woman as a result of artificial insemination, with consent of her husband, is considered to be the legitimate child of the husband and wife." I expressly revoke and withhold my consent for any artificial insemination of my wife in connection with the surrogate arrangement and recognize that by doing so I cannot be declared or considered to be the legal father of said child.

On November 22, 1981, a female child was born, and three days later the trial court dismissed the paternity action. The Court of Appeals upheld the trial judge's opinion that "neither the law nor the facts in this case support the Attorney General's argument that a child conceived and born of Mrs. Appleyard during the marriage is conclusively presumed to be the legitimate child of her husband." Nevertheless the relief requested was beyond the scope of the Paternity Act's general purpose to provide support for a child "born out of wedlock," which did not contemplate or encompass the monetary transaction proposed in this case. The action was therefore dismissed for lack of jurisdiction. But on further appeal, the Supreme Court considered this conclusion to be wrong, since it required "an impossibly restrictive and unnecessary interpretation of the statutory language."

In the Kentucky case of *In re Baby Girl* (1983), a similar problem of statutory interpretation arose regarding the presumption of legitimacy of a child born within a marriage.[4] This was an action by a surrogate mother and her husband seeking to terminate their parental rights and to acknowledge the sponsoring father's legal relation to the child. The court refused to recognize any relationship between the "alleged biological father" and the child in an "alleged" surrogacy arrangement. It stated that "the mere affidavit as to artificial insemination without other positive proof of non-access [of the surrogate's husband] and blood grouping is not sufficient for this court to assume and adjudge the donor [*sic*] to be the natural and biological father of the child." If the presumption that a married woman's husband is the father of her child is conclusive, the only means to establish the legal parenthood of the biological father in a surrogacy situation is through adoption.

Where the surrogate mother is unmarried, problems of a slightly different nature arise in the context of the artificial insemination statutes, which normally speak in terms of "a wife," "a married woman," "the husband of the mother," and the like. The use of artificial insemination to achieve pregnancy in a woman who wishes to bear and rear a child as a single parent is a matter of some controversy. This is due in part to the medical monopoly over the technique (sanctioned in many jurisdictions by legislation that requires a licensed physician for its administration[5]) and the medical focus on male infertility as the primary indication for the procedure. In general terms, indeed, the restriction of access to reproductive technology on criteria of medical indications raises problems of defining infertility, since childlessness often stems from social and economic factors. Is an impotent man, or one with low sperm count, to be considered infertile? Or a woman who is prone to miscarriage and unwilling to bring her pregnancy to term by hospitalization? Or a woman who does not have a mating partner or the economic resources to raise a child on her own? Or a person who has a homosexual preference?[6] Of course, the omission of the unmarried woman from artificial insemination statutes can be understood in light of their general purpose to clarify the child's legitimacy in the typical case confronting the medical practioner: a married couple resorting to artificial insemination with donor sperm. The determination of the child's legal relation to a male person would not ordinarily arise in the case of an unmarried woman who, in choosing to conceive with sperm from (one may assume) an anonymous donor, implicitly expresses her intention to raise a "fatherless" child. The omission also reflects a reluctance to condone extramarital reproductive activity officially. The outcome is, however, that the unmarried woman's right of access to the procedure is uncertain.[7]

It is, therefore, not at all clear whether a medical professional may facilitate a surrogacy arrangement with an unmarried woman even in the absence of expressly prohibitive legislation.[8] Nonetheless, it might be easier to establish the legal relation of biological father and child in the case of an unmarried surrogate mother than in that of a married surrogate. For example, in the New Jersey case of *C.M. v. C.C.*—the only judicial decision to date regarding rights with respect to a child conceived by an unmarried woman through artificial insemination—the court acknowledged the biological father's desire "to take upon himself the responsibility of being a father to a child he is responsible for helping to conceive."[9] If the surrogate is not married, there is no legal presumption of paternity of another man to bar the biological father's application for acknowledgment of his own paternity.[10] In practice, however, there appears to be a preference to employ as surrogates married women who have already borne children, since, presumably, these women have proven themselves physically capable of childbearing and are less likely to rescind the agreement and keep the child than a childless single woman.

Surrogacy and Adoption

The difficulty of reconciling surrogacy arrangements with adoption laws was the basis for the New Jersey Supreme Court's decision to invalidate the surrogacy agreement in the *Baby M* case. The trial court there took the position that the statutory scheme of adoption ought not to be applied to a surrogacy situation that the legislature had not contemplated. But under existing law, adoption provides the only formal means to establish a legal parent-child relation other than on the basis of biological connection. The adoption process, moreover, is in any event necessary to establish the legal relation of the sponsoring wife to the child.

The existing law of reproduction is composed of the common law regarding illegitimacy and the statutory modifications concerning adoption and artificial insemination. If these norms are considered exhaustive and are construed in strict accord with their original intent and purpose, then all social relations of reproduction that do not fall within their scope are illegitimate. In the prelegislative days of artificial insemination this consequence was avoided by pretending that the child had been conceived in the normal course of marriage. This pragmatic solution is unfeasible in a surrogacy situation, short of the surrogate mother fraudulently registering in the hospital under the commissioning wife's name at the time of birth." The dissociation of biological from social parenthood is difficult to conceal or disguise when dealing with a woman who is giving birth to the child.

Monetary surrogate mother agreements are incompatible with three specific types of provisions in adoption statutes: (1) the prohibition in some jurisdictions of nonagency placement; (2) the rules and policies regulating monetary payment in connection with adoption; and (3) the principle of postnatal consent to adoption.

Nonagency Placement

Of these three impediments, restrictions on independent placement can be overcome relatively easily. Most jurisdictions that allow only agency placement also provide an exception in the case of adoption by a blood relative.[12] Thus even if the biological father has to adopt the child to establish legal paternity, his very blood relation to the child is enough to bring the case within the intrafamily exception to the agency placement rule. Where there is no express statutory exception, judicial interpreation could achieve the same result on grounds that the need for a mother or father to adopt their biological child was not considered, and its absence from the statutory scheme was therefore an unintended legislative omission.[13]

Nonetheless, the *In re Baby Girl* Kentucky court refused to admit the motion of a surrogate mother and her husband to terminate their parental rights because the arrangements for the child's placement did not comply with statutory licensing requirements.[14] As mentioned, the court had refused also to acknowledge the alleged biological relation of the commissioning husband to the child. Recognition of that relation is a necessary condition for the intrafamily exception to the agency placement norm. The apparent purpose of the licensing requirements, which include investigation of parental suitability, is to insure that the courts do not endorse relinquishment of responsibility for a child without adequate provision for the child's care by another person. Where termination is sought as part of a surrogacy agreement, these considerations might be impertinent. Not only is there an identifiable biological father who is seeking to assume responsibility for the child, but it is arguable that he has a legal right to do so—stemming, at the very least, from his biological relation to the child if not, too, from his contractual expectations.

Baby Selling

As to the second impediment in adoption law, involving the monetary element, in *Doe v. Kelley* (1980) parties to a surrogacy agreement asked the Michigan Court of Appeals to declare unconstitutional those sections of an adoption statute that prohibited payment of money beyond expenses related to pregnancy, so as to enjoin law enforcement officials from prosecuting them for violating the law.[15] The trial court had held that surrogate motherhood for a fee was tantamount to baby bartering, the social evils of which were, it said, self-evident whether the parties were strangers or friends. "Mercenary considerations used to create a parent-child relationship and its [*sic*] impact on the family unit strikes at the very foundation of human society and is patently and necessarily injurious to the community."[16]

On appeal it was argued, among other things, that the statute was intended to prevent commercial considerations from affecting a mother's decision to consent to her child's adoption. But there was a crucial distinction between payment given pursuant to the sale of a child and payment given in consideration for the time and effort expended by a surrogate mother, who had exercised her choice before conception out of a desire to give another infertile woman the opportunity of raising a child biologically related to her spouse. The appellate court responded clearly and concisely to this argument. Although the decision to have a child was a fundamental interest protected by the constitutional right of privacy, it was not beyond the scope of state interference. The statute did not directly prohibit the sponsoring husband and the surrogate mother from having the child as planned. Instead it precluded payment of money in conjunction with use of the state's adoption procedures. The intention to use the adoption law to change the legal status of the child was not protected by the right to privacy.

This implies that the childless couple's right to privacy does not include a right to effectuate their reproductive decisions. Where the state defines legitimacy and also monopolizes the means to change that status, the right to privacy—as a matter of decision-making authority—is rendered meaningless. Indeed, this is consonant with Supreme Court rulings that deny pregnant women the right to state-funded abortions.[17] The state exercises vicarious control over the means of abortion by licensing a medical monopoly of the procedure. And an indigent woman's right to make an abortion decision lacks substance if she does not have the resources to carry out her decision.

This restriction of private decision-making authority affects not only the sponsoring couple but also the surrogate mother, as to her agreement to relinquish legal maternity. To include surrogacy within the scope of the baby barter ban is to reactivate and reinforce the state's power to define what constitutes legitimate and illegitimate reproduction. To exclude surrogacy from the baby barter prohibition is to transfer that power to the discretion of the individual, to recognize a woman's legal authority to make decisions regarding the exercise of her reproductive capacity, and to change the legal position of other persons on the basis of mutual agreement.

In a later case in the same jurisdiction, *Yates v. Keane* (1987), a trial court refused to enforce a surrogacy agreement, finding it to be a purported contract for the sale and purchase of a child.[18] Considering the dangers of exploiting children for monetary reasons, as well as the misery of infertile couples and the willingness of women to act as surrogates, it went without saying, the court stated, that surrogacy denigrates human dignity. Even if the agreement was characterized as one for personal services only, the Thirteenth Amendment, which banned slavery, would bar specific performance.[19]

But courts in two other jurisdictions took a different position. In the *Matter of Adoption of Baby Girl, L.J.* (1986) a New York court

upheld an adoption in a surrogacy arrangement on grounds of the
best interests of the child, as well as the payment of money to the
surrogate on the ground that the legislature had not contemplated surrogacy when it passed the baby-selling statute.[20] And the Supreme
Court of Kentucky in *Surrogate Parenting Assocs. v. Common-
wealth ex rel. Armstrong* (1986) held that "fundamental differences"
placed surrogacy beyond the reach of the baby-selling statute, since
the surrogacy agreement is entered into before conception and is not
directed at avoiding the consequences of an unwanted pregnancy.[21]
This was an action brought by the attorney general seeking to enjoin
the operation of a surrogacy agency.[22] The trial court had dismissed
the action, characterizing the surrogacy arrangement as a transaction
between the surrogate mother and the "natural father" by which he
pays her to carry the child and relinquish parental rights. "How," it
queried, "can a natural father be characterised as either adopting or
buying his own baby? . . . He does not [and cannot] buy the right
to adopt a child with which he already has a legal relationship."

The distinction between the sale of a child and the sale of reproductive services might appear, at first glance, to be a matter of se-
mantics, but in fact it captures a vital difference between surrogacy
and adoption. In surrogacy, conception is deliberate, the persons
who wish to assume the social responsibility for rearing the child are
clearly identifiable from the outset, and the intention to dissociate
biological and legal parenthood is manifest. One of the reasons for
the baby barter ban is, as I have already pointed out, to protect birth
mothers from the monetary enticement of unscrupulous baby mon-
gers that may influence her to make a decision to alienate her "natural" right to the child. Even allowing the soundness of this paternalistic approach in the case of a woman terminating a parental
relation to a child conceived unintentionally, it may well be urged
that it is inappropriate in the case of surrogacy. If the purpose is to
insure the voluntariness of the decision, attention should focus on
the parties' negotiations before conception. If conception is intentional and the surrogate mother is an autonomous agent, she will
presumably weigh the various implications of her voluntary reproductive activity before entering any agreement.[23]

Postnatal Consent

Although the Kentucky Supreme Court refrained from finding the monetary element illegal, it also concluded that consent to terminate parental rights before conception was unenforceable when statutes provide that such consent is invalid before five days after birth. Even though the agreement might be a legal contract, the surrogate mother had the right to void the contract if she changed her mind during pregnancy or immediately after birth. According to this approach, even if surrogacy does not constitute a criminal offense, it is not legal in the weaker sense that the agreement—in and of itself—has no effect on the parties' legal relations. Even if the surrogate mother intends all along to relinquish the child, legal parenthood is vested in her at birth. If she withdraws her consent to adoption within the lawful period, her legal relation to the child cannot be severed, and the interests or expectations of the sponsoring parents are unprotected.

In one case the surrogate mother changed her mind during the pregnancy. Rather than sue for breach of contract, the sponsoring couple filed a paternity action and a motion to determine custody and visitation rights. Eventually the parties reached an out-of-court settlement according to which the surrogate gained custody and the sponsoring husband was named as the father on the child's birth certificate but did not retain any visitation rights.[24] And in a British case, A v. C, (1985) which involved a surrogate mother "on the fringe" of prostitution, the agreement was deemed unenforceable on grounds of the public policy against baby selling, the surrogate received custody, and the father was denied visitation rights.[25]

The rule that defers the coming into effect of consent to adoption until after the child's birth is designed, like the baby barter ban, to insure the voluntary nature of such consent. Whether it is pertinent in the case of surrogacy relations is again questionable in view of the deliberate nature of conception. The surrogate mother could be expected to weigh the prospective investment in her birthing labor before agreeing to the arrangement. If her initial agreement is voluntary, why should she not be held responsible for the consequences of her autonomous reproductive decision so as to fulfill the expectations of the other parties to the contract?

Moreover, the policy of postnatal consent is part of a *closed* adoption scheme in which termination of parental rights has the radical effect of severing any social relation between the birth mother and her child. But this need not be the case in surrogacy. The relations could be open, allowing the surrogate liberal visitation rights to the child while custody vests in the sponsoring parents. Indeed, this was the practical outcome of *Baby M,* except that the court invalidated the surrogate's initial consent to adoption by the sponsoring wife. There does not, however, appear to be any logical impediment to allowing visitation while technically terminating the surrogate's parental rights and acknowledging the legal relation of the sponsoring wife to the child. Under *Baby M,* moreover, the legal parenthood of the child is divided between biological father and mother, placing the conflicting parties in an ongoing relationship of shared responsibilities that neither contemplated at the time of their initial agreement. It might well be wiser to establish clearly that the sponsoring couple have full parental authority over the child, subject to the surrogate's right of visitation.

The Unwanted Child

So far we have been dealing with a situation in which both parties to a surrogacy arrangement want custody of the child. But the most tragic breakdown in surrogacy relations will occur when *neither* party wants to assume responsibility for the child. This problem arose in unfortunate circumstances in 1983, when a deformed baby boy was born in Michigan to a surrogate mother and neither she nor the sponsoring husband wanted responsibility for his care. At first, the sponsoring husband directed physicians to discontinue treatment of the baby's medical condition, but the hospital obtained court permission to care for him. Later on, blood tests showed that the sponsoring husband was not the biological father. It appeared that the surrogate had failed to observe a term of the agreement to abstain from sexual relations with her husband at the time of artificial insemination. The surrogate's husband was established to be the biological father, and the couple subsequently decided to keep the child.[26]

The problem of the unwanted child is obviously not unique to surrogacy relations. If a child is conceived in the normal way legal responsibility attaches to the biological parents whether they like it or not, although they can divest themselves of their legal parenthood through adoption. According to *Baby M,* legal parenthood vests in the surrogate mother at birth despite the prior-to-conception intentions of the parties to establish legal parenthood in the sponsoring couple. The surrogate's right to change her mind and keep the child thus implies her legal responsibility for an unwanted child. Whereas a less than perfect baby may be accepted as fate in the normal course of having children, a more callous attitude may show itself in surrogacy situations.[27] But the case in which neither party wants the child raises precisely the same issue as that in which both parties seek custody: the determination of legal parenthood in surrogacy relations. If the prior-to-conception intentions are binding on the parties and the sponsoring couple's legal parent-child relation to the child is acknowledged, then they would be attached with legal responsibility subject to divestment through adoption.

Legislative Response

Until the *Baby M* case made international headlines and brought the complexity of surrogacy to the public consciousness, bills for regulating these relations had been introduced in only five legislatures in the United States. One bill in Michigan sought to criminalize surrogacy out of concern for the "sexual" exploitation of surrogate mothers as "mercenary baby-making factories" and to prevent the exposure of "made-to-order" babies to unacceptable standards of perfection.[28] The other bills allowed payment to the surrogate mother "for the purpose of compensating her for her services," "for loss of work time," "for loss of income directly related to the pregnancy," "as the parties to the contract consider appropriate," and subject to court approval.[29] These bills all proposed in one way or another that the sponsoring couple be presumed the legal parents of the child at birth but also allowed the surrogate to revoke her consent to the arrangement within a prescribed statutory period.

Following the *Baby M* trial court's decision to enforce the surrogacy agreement, however, a wave of legislative initiatives sought to regulate surrogacy relations. Seventy bills were introduced in twenty-seven states, and even though the federal government usually defers to the states on family issues, three bills were introduced in Congress: one seeking to ban surrogacy, one to forbid enforcement of the agreements in federal courts, and one to bar the use of federal funds in helping veterans form families through surrogate mothers. Twenty-one of the state bills were designed either to ban surrogacy completely or to outlaw payment to the surrogate mother. The others proposed various safeguards for protecting the interests of the concerned parties, including requirements for psychological screening of surrogate mother candidates, proof of the sponsoring mother's infertility, licensing of lawyers and doctors involved in arranging surrogacy agreements, court approval of the arrangement, and statutory periods for the surrogate to revoke her consent after birth.[30]

The Law of Contract

The general thesis I am suggesting in this work is that the legal consequences of surrogacy, and reproductive collaboration in general, should be determined as a matter of contract in accordance with the expressed intention of the parties before conception. In this scheme legal parenthood becomes a matter of autonomous agreement regardless of the parties' gender. Indeed, the absence of express statutory regulation of surrogacy can be construed as allowing recourse to the general rules of contract law, the legal machinery by which, broadly speaking, the performance of services by some members of the community for others is carried out.[31] Accordingly, a surrogacy arrangement can be characterized generally as a contract for the sale of personal reproductive services. Since the purpose of the contract is to produce a new human being—to be regarded in accord with Kantian principle as an end in itself rather than a means to the end of others—the agreement must be further qualified as a contract for the benefit of a third party, the child. This does not necessarily mean that the child is vested with any rights or interests, either prenatally or postnatally, but rather that legal responsibility for its care and nurture should be imposed conclusively in accord with the parties' agreement as a matter of the child's best interests.

Generally speaking, the law provides that an agreement will not give rise to legal consequences (that is, will not amount to a contract) if the parties did not intend to bind themselves as a matter of law. Courts often refuse to enforce promises of a domestic nature on this ground, although a general reluctance to intervene in familial relations is as much a factor in their reticence as any factual finding in a specific case that the parties did not intend to be legally bound by their promises.[32] Courts will also refuse to enforce an agreement if the parties fail to comply with a number of formalities which, when in fact complied with, are taken to be evidence of the mutual intention to create a legally binding relationship. In the common law the main formal requirement is that of "consideration." A one-sided promise does not, as a rule, constitute a contract. The meeting of the minds must be demonstrated by some kind of reciprocal exchange. Where the contract is such that only one party undertakes to perform an act, the consideration given by the other party is normally in the form of monetary payment.

In some cases all the formal requirements are satisifed, but the agreement is without legal effect because the law disapproves of its purpose or the manner in which it seeks to achieve that purpose and will not sully its hands in assisting its effectuation. Thus an illegal or immoral purpose will render a contract void and unenforceable. The same applies where the object of the agreement is considered to be in conflict with a public interest, or against public policy.[33]

A surrogacy agreement, under which the surrogate mother promises to bear and birth a child and the sponsoring couple promises to pay her for her services, would appear to comply with the formal requirement of consideration. The interests of the child as third-party beneficiary are met by the undertaking of the sponsoring parents to assume responsibility for the infant after birth.[34] But a surrogacy agreement could be void on grounds of illegality under the criminal prohibition of payment in connection with adoption. What is more, if the statutory law of adoption is construed to cover also surrogacy, the requirement of postnatal consent would prevent the formation of a contract because no pregnant woman could be legally bound to a prenatal commitment as regards her child's placement after birth, which is the essence of surrogacy. In this case there would be no consideration for the sponsoring parents' part in the agreement. Assuming, though, that surrogacy presents a distinctive situation not governed by adoption law, is there any rule of public policy that would prevent the surrogate mother from making a legally effective commitment toward the sponsoring parents?

The law of contract stigmatizes several categories of agreements as contrary to public policy,[35] including contracts prejudicial to family relations and, in particular, an agreement by a parent to renounce his or her rights in relation to a child. One rationale is that parent-child relations are a matter of legal status, independent of the parties' agreement. Another rationale is that some positions in society entail obligations that cannot be divested simply by means of contract. Whereas the argument for the surrogate mother's incapacity to enter a binding contract is usually based on her "natural right" to the fruit of her womb, the present point illuminates her responsibility for the child. The question is not, however, whether the surrogate may renounce her parental status without further ado but whether she may transfer that status to other responsible adults before conception.

Even if the contract is regarded as one for the sale of reproductive services rather than for the sale of a child, the question remains whether monetary factors might unduly influence the surrogate mother. In contract law undue influence may be pleaded to avoid what otherwise seems to be a valid contract in order to redress an unfair balance in the parties' bargaining positions. Courts are, however, reluctant to admit a plea that the contract was made unfairly since in general the law treats all persons as being of equal contracting capacity.[36]

A recent psychological study of surrogate mothers indicates that, given proper counseling, prohibition of monetary payment is not necessary for competent consent. (Counseling was given with respect to two decisions: to participate in the surrogacy arrangement and to select the sponsoring parents on a model of open adoption. Accordingly, it addressed the surrogate candidate's motivation, her potential psychological response to the pregnancy and relinquishment, and the nature and extent of the relationship she desired with the sponsoring parents after birth.) The study found that although financial gain was an element in the motivation to enter a surrogacy agreement, it was complemented by additional factors: the desire to be pregnant as an enjoyable experience independent of the anticipation of raising a child, the satisfaction of giving a child to an infertile couple, and the need to repeat a previous experience of losing a child through abortion or adoption so as to master an act that the surrogate felt she had less control of originally. Furthermore, the surrogates did not think of the fee (paid in a lump sum after delivery) as payment in exchange for parental rights but as a fee for services rendered. Payment became less important as the pregnancy progressed, and the significant determinant appeared to be the development of an idealized empathetic relationship with the sponsoring couple, toward whom the surrogate usually developed a sense of duty. Cooperation in the legal process of terminating parental rights continued well after receipt of the surrogacy fee.[37]

The model of a contract for personal services focuses on the social relations of the autonomous reproducing adults. The surrogacy agreement can be characterized as a contract for the sale of a baby only if we abstract the resulting child out of this social context. Indeed this view leads to the callous and offensive implication that the child is a kind of consumer product. Even if the sole motivation to sell reproductive services is financial, still the child cannot be treated as a commodity, subject, supposedly, to the general rules governing the sale of goods. This is clearly unacceptable. For example, one of these rules provides that if the goods fail in any respect to conform to the contract, the buyer may reject or accept the whole or any part of the goods.[38] The notion of designer kids, made to order with various specifications and rejected when not born as warranted, haunts and captures our imagination. But the rules regulating the sale of goods have their source in the gradual development of case law during the nineteenth century, which elaborated the duties of buyer and seller on the basis of their presumed intentions. If these rules are inappropriate in the surrogacy context, that need not be taken to reflect upon the general impropriety of such relations but rather to indicate the contrary intentions of the parties. Classification of surrogacy agreements as contracts for the sale of a child might indeed result in the child being treated as a commodity.[39] If, however, the dominant feature of these relations is perceived as the sale of the surrogate mother's personal services, in accordance with the parties' intentions, then different rules would apply—for instance, that the right to the personal services cannot be transferred to a third party.

If there is no necessary logical inference of social responsibility for a child from the fact of biological connection, a principle of personal autonomy would allow the individual to determine its normative consequences. Legal parenthood could be presumed on grounds of biology as an efficient default rule for insuring that children are generally taken care of, but it could be rebutted by evidence that the collaborating adults intended otherwise. If autonomy is understood as the deliberate exercise of choice with respect to the individual's reproductive capacity, the point at which the parties' intentions should be established is before conception, for it is the deliberacy of the effort to conceive a new life that gives rise to responsibility for the results of that effort. Where conception is not rationally planned but occurs as an unintended consequence of sexual intercourse, the default presumption would apply to vest responsibility in the biological parents. But where two or more individuals contrive rationally to reproduce a child, their intentions can be the source of responsibility for the consequences of their collaboration.

As regards the interests of the child, the principal concern should be that from the moment of conception there be at least one clearly identifiable adult who will be responsible for the child. That person need not have any biological relation to the child, and conversely the biological parent need not have any legal connection with her. So long as conception has not occurred the parties may rescind their part in the agreement. But if reproduction is to be responsible, the relations should be conclusively established at conception so as to avoid displacement of the child in a custody dispute after birth. The normative parent-child relation would thus be established through autonomous agreement, and to the extent that biological parents do not assume responsibility for the child they would be regarded as providing reproductive services to the social parents.

CHAPTER 6

In Vitro Fertilization—
The Objectification of Motherhood

What is this life by which you, who exist still incomplete,
count for more than I, who exist complete already? . . .
What do you think I am: a container, a jar, where you put
some object for safekeeping?
—*Oriana Fallaci,* Letter to a Child Never Born

In vitro fertilization is a noncoital method of conception whereby an egg is fertilized with sperm in the laboratory and then implanted for gestation in the uterus. Children conceived by this means are popularly called test tube babies, referring to the petri dish in which fertilization occurs. The first child conceived through in vitro fertilization was born in 1978 after twenty years of research by a British team. Over two hundred in vitro clinical programs currently operate throughout the world with over one thousand live births every year.

A contractual model for defining parent-child relations would appear to be suited to the various forms of reproductive collaboration afforded by this technique. That model is, however, based on the perception of women as autonomous agents, whereas the history of the development of in vitro fertilization indicates that medical attitudes are still very much informed by the patriarchal idea of women as passive support organisms that are secondary to the value of the human life that they produce. Arguably, a change in reproductive consciousness along the lines of a contractual surrogacy model is, therefore, all the more necessary.

Woman as Human Subject of Research

Although Britain's Warnock Committee devoted an entire chapter of its report to the ethics of research on human embryos, expressing concern about the moral rights involved, in no way did it address the status of women as subjects of scientific experimentation.[1] Indeed, by defining embryo research as excluding "new and untried treatment, undertaken during the attempt to alleviate the infertility of a particular patient," it voices a prevailing attitude that ne v reproductive procedures are experimental as regards the embr /fetus but therapeutic for the infertile couple.[2] This resulted in the pai icipating women being classified as patients rather than humai subjects of medical experimentation.

A 1979 report of the Ethics Advisory Board to the U. . Department of Health, Education, and Welfare on in vitro fertiliza on focused similarly on the moral status of the embryo and the pr ection of potential human life, including discussion of possible ca ses of action on behalf of an injured child and "the crime of feticide." In summary it also noted among the more difficult ethical issues the safety and efficacy of the procedure and the potential long-range adverse effects of research, but here too the main concern was for the physical and mental health of resulting children. As for the mother, the board expressed concern about the efficacy of a procedure that had produced only three successes to date but made no comment on the fact that access to women's bodies was necessary to validate and improve the new reproductive technique. The report disposed of "still unanswered questions of safety for [the] mother" with the observation that "many women have told the Board that in order to bear a child of their own they will submit to whatever risks are involved." Although it suggested that information regarding safety and health should be developed and disseminated so that fully informed choices could be made, the board did not propose any restriction on research until such information was available. And like the Warnock Committee, it made no express mention of women as subjects of research but coupled them with their husbands as patients in therapy.[3]

Ovum donors and surrogate mothers could not be regarded as patients, however, since they would not benefit from the treatment. The Ethics Advisory Board considered that regulations to protect the health of ovum donors might be adopted but suggested that surrogacy could be prohibited on the ground that "service as a surrogate mother is an unacceptable form of employment."[4] It gave no thought to the possibility of employing surrogate mothers without compensation, and the need for their protection in such case.

The distinction between the experimental nature of a reproductive technique (for the embryo) and its therapeutic nature (for the mother) stems from the general state of mind that isolates the egg/embryo as a separate, independent entity from the human context of the reproducing woman as a person-subject. Thus the American Medical Association—in a somewhat confusing statement to the Ethics Advisory Board—recognized that in vitro fertilization was experimental and in the same breath suggested that "the patient" should be informed accordingly of the risks and alternatives. It considered the technique to be "one mechanism, among others, of human artificial insemination" and concluded that it should be available on the same terms and conditions as "other *medically acceptable* mechanisms of artificial insemination" (emphasis added). Interestingly enough, artificial insemination—a method that overcomes *male* infertility— was presented as a procedure that had enabled *women* to bear children and overcome "natural impediments to conception" and "frustration of a basic biological drive."[5]

The failure to recognize the woman as a human subject of research is inconsistent with generally accepted ethical principles. According to these, there is a distinction between "research" (designed to develop or contribute to generalizable knowledge) and "practice" (designed *solely* to enhance the well-being of an individual patient). Although the distinction becomes blurred when research is aimed at evaluating the safety and efficacy of a particular innovative therapy, the general rule is that if there is any element of research in an activity it should undergo review for the protection of human subjects.[6]

Informed consent is required for both experimental research and therapeutic practice, but agreement seems nearly universal that consent to the investigator-subject relationship should meet higher standards than those for the physician-patient relationship. The autonomy of the subject or patient is the general ethical principle that underlies the requirement of informed consent, and there is consid-

108 In Vitro Fertilization

erable debate as to whether a treating physician can at all negotiate fairly with a patient to become a subject of research. This is because the very nature of the patient role tends to limit a person's autonomy vis-à-vis the physician, since one cannot get better by a mere act of will and is inherently dependent on professional help. Indeed, patients who present themselves as willing to take any risk for even a remote possibility of relief are considered seriously vulnerable subjects of research. One may well include in this category infertile women who desperately want a child.[7]

Clearly, under existing social conditions a woman's sense of self-esteem and of value to others hinges greatly on her role as mother, and she can be expected therefore to overextend herself in cooperating with doctors so as to fulfill that role for herself and her mate. In such circumstances she depends on the physician's esoteric scientific expertise and is likely to be intimidated by it. She may be afraid to appear stupid by asking questions that challenge the physician's wisdom, and she may fear that a refusal to cooperate at any stage of the treatment will jeopardize her relationship with the physician. The childless woman's high degree of motivation to participate in experimental procedures should be regarded as indicative of her special vulnerability as a subject of research rather than as grounds for leniency with respect to the general safeguards protecting human subjects.

The principal mechanism for the protection of human subjects of medical research under federal regulations is the hospital internal review board. The rationale for establishing an independent body to be responsible for determining whether research fulfills ethical standards is that the investigators themselves are always in a position of potential conflict between the pursuit of scientific knowledge and the welfare of the human subjects of their research.[8]

The regulations also lay down several criteria for internal review board approval of research. In particular, special protection must be provided when the research proposal exceeds "minimal risk," defined so that "the risks of harm anticipated . . . are not greater, considering probability and magnitude, than those ordinarily encountered in daily life or during the performance of routine physical or psychological examinations."[9] Where the minimal risk threshold is exceeded, for example, the subject must be informed whether compensation or medical treatment will be available if injury occurs.[10] It may be assumed that any woman participating in experimental reproductive programs that involve bodily intrusion is subject to more than minimal risk as defined above.

The same regulations contain a special section addressing "additional protections pertaining to research, development and related activities involving fetuses, pregnant women and human in vitro fertilisation." In fact, the woman is mentioned expressly as a human subject in only one place, to the effect that a pregnant woman may not be involved in this research unless the purpose is to meet her health needs and the fetus will be placed at minimum relative risk or unless the risk to the fetus is absolutely minimal. This is one instance of the general tendency to apply a double standard of what constitutes acceptable bodily intrusion and attendant risk when the subject is women's reproductive activity.[11] Aside from this restriction on a pregnant woman's activity (out of concern for the fetus), women in general, as subjects in their own right, receive no special attention. There is no mention of nonpregnant women participating in experimental procedures aimed at achieving conception. Nor is any distinction made between intrauterine and extrauterine fetal experimentation as regards the mother's informed consent, despite the qualitative difference in her involvement. In both cases she is merely coupled with the father in this regard.[12]

Experimentation on human beings was conducted without sufficient controlled animal research.[13] When the first in vitro child was born in 1978, fewer than two hundred rabbits, two hundred mice, and fifty rats had been born under the procedure. A second child was born that year from the same British project; at the time 68 women had participated in the team's research. The third child was born in 1980 in Australia, bringing the score to three normal births from 278 participating women. When the first clinic opened in the United States in 1979, the experimental nature of the program was acknowledged, but it was also referred to as a service to infertile couples. The "patients" were expected to pay the laboratory expenses and hospital charges, although professional fees were waived.[14]

The primary medical indication for the procedure is to circumvent blockage in the fallopian tubes, which accounts for approximately 40 percent of cases of female infertility. In such cases, the woman has typically normal ovulation and is capable of sustaining a pregnancy, but the blockage prevents passage of mature eggs to the womb for fertilization. Success rates are often cited in terms of pregnancy per egg retrieval, but not all attempts at retrieval actually recover mature eggs and not all pregnancies result in live births.[15] If the success rate is presented as between 15 and 25 percent, this means a 75 to 85 percent failure rate.

The technique originally used to obtain eggs was laparoscopy, which involved inserting a fiber optics surgical instrument through a small cut in the abdomen to allow inspection of internal organs under general anesthesia.[16] To achieve successful fertilization the egg had to be retrieved at the specific moment in the ovulatory cycle corresponding with the maturation that normally occurs before the egg's release from the ovary follicles. Hormonal treatment induced superovulation in the woman so that several eggs (as many as twelve at a time) could be retrieved with one surgical exploration.[17]

The laparoscopy was only one stage in the process. Before admission to an in vitro fertilization program there were a number of preliminary procedures that came under the heading of the "infertility workup." Male factors of infertility—which account for approximately half the instances of childlessness—could be identified easily at an early stage through observing sperm quality and quantity. The rigorous part of the workup started only after these observations failed to disclose a disorder in the male partner. The woman was instructed, first, to monitor her menstrual cycle through daily records of basal body temperature and to program her sexual activity accordingly over a period of several months.[18] If having intercourse in the right way at the right time did not produce pregnancy, painful diagnostic procedures were employed to determine the cause of infertility. Hormonal therapy would be indicated for an ovulatory problem, but one apparently major complication—hyperstimulation of the ovary, which is life threatening in severe cases—was rarely mentioned. Blocked tubes could be opened by forcing pressurized liquid through them, a painful procedure that might have to be administered every one to two months to maintain an opening. Ovulation had to be determined precisely before attempting egg retrieval. One method was based on detection of hormonal indications in the woman's urine, and she was instructed to urinate a determined amount every three hours, which required control of her fluid intake.[19]

When it was decided that the woman was ovulating, she was rushed into the operating room for the laparoscopy. One medical description of this procedure did not refer to the woman at all, focusing instead on the technical aspects of obtaining an unharmed egg.

> The ovaries must be clearly accessible for the collection of mature eggs. . . . The ovary is held by forceps that have been introduced into the abdominal cavity adjacent to the laparoscope so that one or more of its egg follicles can be gently punctured and aspirated under vision by a special 23cm long needle which is inserted between the laparoscope and the forceps. This needle is lined by teflon tubing which is continuous with the collecting test-tube, so that the flow of follicular fluid is constant, and turbulence is reduced. This needle and collecting system allows an egg collection rate of 90 percent and reduces the risk of damage to the egg in its passage from the ovary to the collecting tube.[20]

The obscurity of the woman as human subject had dire consequences. Lesley Brown, the mother of the first child conceived through in vitro fertilization, could not afford the cost of a one-day stay in hospital to recuperate from laparoscopy. She began bleeding as soon as she got on the train home. This is how she described the experience: "The blood started to seep through my thick woolen dress. . . . I held my coat tightly around me, so no one would see. We changed trains four times on the journey to Bristol, and at one station, I was crying so much that John picked me up and carried me in his arms from one end of the platform to the next."[21]

She and her husband were not initially informed about the experimental nature of the treatment. Nor did they fully understand until late in her pregnancy that human in vitro fertilization had never been successfully performed. In her words again:

> I didn't remember [the physician] saying his method of produc-
> ing babies had ever worked, and I certainly didn't ask. I just
> imagined that hundreds of children had already been born
> through being conceived outside their mothers' wombs. Having
> a baby was all that mattered. It didn't seem strange that I had
> never read about anyone who had had a child in that way be-
> fore. I could understand their mothers wanting to keep quiet
> afterwards about how their children had been started off. It just
> didn't occur to me that it would almost be a miracle if it worked
> with me.[22]

The woman's physical ardor and the emotional havoc of hopes being repeatedly raised and dashed was overlooked. The procedure by which eggs are obtained is often referred to as harvesting, farm-ing, hunting, and the like, as if the woman who submits to its con-suing demands is a passive organism, a field yielding its natural crop after being fertilized and cultivated in the hormonal agriculture of medical technology. The heroes of the battle against infertility are thus the doctors who invent the means of combat rather than the women whose persons provide the fields for scientific engagement. Their submissive participation is taken for granted to such an extent that their situation as human subjects of medical experimentation goes unnoticed.

The Scientification of Reproduction

This failure to appreciate the status of the infertile woman as a re-search subject is one of the unfortunate consequences of the tradi-tional perception of woman's passive reproductive function and in-deed destiny. The woman's own failure to appreciate her situation is indicative of the all-pervasiveness of that cultural perception. This oversight is part of a historical process in which women's social control of reproduction has been usurped by the medical profession, resulting in scientific objectification of the human reproductive process and its abstraction from the personality of the reproducing adult. The biggest single difference between traditional and contemporary reproductive practice is that the technical knowledge and resources now belong to the medical profession. Today the experts on fertility control are not its users but those who develop and prescribe it. When this is added to the medicalization of birth and child care we have a situation in which reproduction as a human activity is increasingly divorced from sexual and social relations.[23]

Kristin Luker even suggests that the criminalization of abortion in the second half of the nineteenth century was a political move by the medical profession to establish their technical and moral superiority over competing health practitioners, subsequently designated "quacks." In contrast to other medical-moral issues—alcoholism, venereal disease, and prostitution—abortion presented a matter of life and death that allowed physicians to make a symbolic claim of superior moral stature in accord with the Hippocratic Oath. To be trusted with arbitrating the sacred boundary between life and death, professional doctors had to claim both that the embryo was a life and that they could sometimes sacrifice that life.[24] Consequently, the standard abortion statute before the reform of the 1960s established a medical monopoly by including a provision rendering abortion legal only when undertaken by a physician to preserve the life of the mother, as an exception to the general criminal prohibition. What constituted a threat to the mother's life was not specified, nor was there any mechanism for reviewing medical judgment on the matter.

The medicalization of abortion is one instance of the general scientific appropriation of control over reproduction. One effect has been increased technical intervention in the management of childbirth. Thus the hospitalization rate for childbirth in many countries approximates 100 percent, although it has never been proved scientifically that most women and their babies benefit from institutionalized birth.[25] Likewise, the frequency of cesarian-section delivery has doubled each decade since the 1950s (replacing, it is true, other more damaging obstetric operations) and now accounts for 25 percent of hospital deliveries. Although c-sections are three times more frequent in hospital deliveries than in planned home births managed by midwives, the mortality rate for mothers and babies do not differ significantly. Beyond the obvious convenience for medical teams of planned deliveries, one explanation for the rise in hospital c-sections is that medical standards for intervention are dictated by statistical data for the "normal" length of labor, which have decreased from 12.5 hours in 1948 to 8 hours in 1980 for the first stage of labor in first births. Data from home births in the 1970s showed 14.5 hours as the average length of the same.[26] Deference to medical judgement about indications for c-section is heightened because, almost by definition, the laboring woman's life is at stake—she *must* expel the fetus somehow to survive.

Although medicalization has undoubtedly minimized the physical ordeal of childbirth, it has also created an atmosphere of crisis and isolated the laboring woman from the psychical support system that traditional midwivery provided against the emotional stress of birthing. For an intelligent, self-regulating female this may be much more upsetting than the physical concomitants of her condition. In addition, medical experts at times convey confusing messages as to the proper management of pregnancy. The pregnant woman seems to join a competition to produce, as it were, a bigger and better baby but is not really allowed complete freedom of choice since her attending doctor enjoys the final say.[27]

The authority of the doctor over matters of life and death and the opposition this manifests to patient autonomy is not unique to reproductive medicine. But the growing technical power to control prenatal life and the concurrent concern for fetal protection has the effect of obliterating the woman's subjective experience of her reproductive activity. Adrienne Rich describes how this becomes a collective experience of alienation from childbirth.

The hierarchical atmosphere of the hospital, the definition of childbirth as a medical emergency, the fragmentation of body from mind, were the environment in which we gave birth. . . . The experience of lying half-awake in a barred crib, in a labor room with other women moaning in a drugged condition, where "no one comes" except to do a pelvic examination or give an injection, is a classic experience of alienated childbirth. The loneliness, the sense of abandonment, of being imprisoned, powerless, and depersonalized is the chief collective memory of women who have given birth in American hospitals.[28]

Defining Motherhood

The regulation of women's inherent power of giving life by a male-dominated profession—through the medical control of contraception, abortion, obstetrics, gynecology, fertility, and extrauterine reproduction—is an essential element in the patriarchal perception of women as objects rather than subjects in their own right. The tendency in scientific discourse to abstract the social personality of the reproducing woman into an objective "natural" process leads to some confusion when discussing the normative consequences of one particular application of the in vitro fertilization technique.

In vitro fertilization has so far been used mainly to reproduce children who are the genetic offspring of both partners in a previously childless marriage. In this usage, the technique differs from normal childbearing in one respect only: conception is achieved outside the womb. The door is, however, open to other forms of collaborative reproduction. For example, an anovulatory woman could carry the pregnancy of a child conceived with the egg of another woman. Likewise, a woman unable to sustain pregnancy might reproduce a child conceived with her own egg through employing the gestational services of another woman. This implies the differentiation of three factors in female reproductive activity: the genetic, the gestational, and the social.[29] But whereas social, or legal, motherhood has hitherto stemmed automatically from biological motherhood, the separation of the genetic and gestational functions poses the question: Who is to be regarded as the mother of a child conceived with the egg of one woman and carried to term in the womb of another?

Obviously the question "Who is the mother?" cannot be answered as a matter of scientific fact, since the two women are here equally necessary factors in the causal process that results in the child's birth. The tradition that attaches legal parenthood to biological relation does not meet the situation, since both women have a biological connection with the child. The question should, therefore, be rephrased in normative terms: Who *ought* be the person in whose charge the child is to be nurtured after birth? Which of the women *should* be regarded as socially responsible for the child?

Suppose that a woman has contracted with a childless couple to bear a child conceived from their own egg and sperm. What would the law make of the genetic mother's rights vis-à-vis the child? Would the agreement have any legal effect? Under the current law applying to surrogate mothers who provide both genetic and gestational functions, the agreement is unenforceable and the genetic father's rights are overriden by the birth mother's claim to the child. If we extend this rule to the hypothetical, the agreement would not be effective and the genetic mother's rights would be overriden. But can we say that the normative role of the egg differs from that of the sperm?

In discussing the significance of biological parenthood for the definition of a legal parent-child relation, there is a tendency to classify genetic male and female roles as one and the same thing and to oppose them to the exclusively female role of gestation. The genetic mother is likened to the genetic father under the neutral name of "gamete donor," and the value of genetic continuity that underlies their respective claims to legal parenthood is held to concede to the superior value of the gestational mother's incomparable physical and emotional involvement in producing the child-to-be.[30]

For example, Australia's Waller Committee, in discussing "the question of a maternal relationship where donor ova are used," noted that "the law has assumed that the woman who bears a child is always . . . that child's mother." It recommended that the legal status of a child born as a result of the use of donor ova through in vitro fertilization should be the same as in the case of donor sperm in artificial insemination, meaning that the genetic relation should be deprived of any normative or legal consequence.[31]

In similar fashion, Britain's Warnock Committee took the view that "where a woman donates an egg for transfer the donation should

be treated as absolute and . . . like a male donor she should have no
rights or duties with regard to any resulting child." It recommended
that legislation be enacted to provide accordingly that "when a child
is born to a woman following donation of another's egg the woman
giving birth should, for all purposes, be regarded in law as the
mother of that child, and . . . the egg donor should have no rights
or obligations in respect of the child." [32]

If the fact that sperm and egg both provide material for the genetic
constitution of the person-to-be is taken as grounds for the normative
conclusion that the significance of genetic parenthood is one and the
same for male and female, we are adopting a typical "male" point of
view. That conclusion follows from a pragmatist goal-oriented
worldview that places primary value on the end of (re)production
while ignoring the contextual process that leads to the end product.

Biological fatherhood and motherhood differ from each other in
nature and scope far beyond the obvious uniqueness of the female's
gestational capacity. There is only a superficial parallel between the
sperm and egg that combine to form a person's genetic constitution.
The processes by which germinal materials are produced in male and
female differ fundamentally. Female gametes (eggs) are fully formed
at birth and released monthly one at a time during the ovulatory
years, whereas male gametes (sperm) are formed continuously start-
ing at puberty and obtainable in hundreds of millions every three to
four days. Sperm can be obtained at any time through the simple
voluntary and self-controlled method of masturbation, whereas obtaining mature eggs involves a complicated procedure that includes
hormonal therapy and synchronization of the woman's ovulatory
cycle, and culminates in the woman's submission to an intrusive
medical procedure. [33]

Genetic motherhood not only differs essentially from genetic fatherhood but could well be more akin to gestational motherhood.
The hormones that a woman routinely ingests to induce superovulation might effect an experience similar to that of hormonal changes
in pregnancy. And where the process of genetic motherhood culminates in a surgical operation under general anesthesia, it brings to
mind the experience of women in cesarian-section childbirth.

Eggs for donation are often obtained from a woman who is herself undergoing in vitro fertilization therapy, in the course of which she may produce eggs in surplus of her own needs. If the woman's emotional experience is at all considered, it is to invoke the high degree of self-interested motivation that she brings to the procedure and her empathy for the fate of other infertile women. The frustration of the infertile woman is such, it is said, that she will willingly submit to the emotionally exhausting and physically taxing efforts to correct her condition. And being aware of the misery of infertility, she is also willing to donate her surplus eggs to other similarly situated women.[34] The emotional costs involved in obtaining her eggs are thus outweighed by the emotional benefits she gains from the chance to bear her own child.

Note, however, that this analysis was made when in vitro fertilization programs involving donated eggs were at an early experimental stage.[35] As the Waller Committee pointed out, this required special counseling in obtaining an egg donor's informed consent. Noting the patient's special vulnerability, it cautioned that she might be reluctant to disappoint the doctors, scientists, and other patients in the program and advised that counseling deal with the possibility of special disappointment should the donor fail to become pregnant and the recipient succeed.[36]

Further, without depreciating the anguish of the infertile woman, the measure of frustration and benefits reaped from the "egg harvesting" procedure indicates the social pressures exerted on the childless woman in a pronatalist patriarchal culture that regards motherhood as the biological destiny of women and considers women who do not fulfill that destiny as lacking something essential in their social personhood. Indeed, were it not for these cultural pressures, the inability to come to terms with childlessness and the obsessive willingness to submit to most consuming strenuous physical procedures to alleviate that condition might be regarded as neurotic.[37]

Be that as it may, the strong motivation of a woman to bear her own genetic child and her empathetic altruism with respect to surplus genetic material do not appear to lead to any normative conclusion as to the relative significance of genetic and gestational motherhood. That is, they seem to beg the question of how one resolves competing claims to social motherhood, unless taken to indicate the woman's prior-to-conception intentions as regards the social responsibility for the child-to-be. Moreover, the psychology of the infertile woman gives us no indiction of how to deal with a perfectly healthy reproducing female who, for example, gave (or sold) an egg to a friend.

Indeed, the question "Who is the mother?" cannot be answered simplistically by labeling reproductive roles according to objective biological function and must be addressed with an eye to the particular social relations that engendered the reproductive collaboration. The primacy given to gestational motherhood assumes a situation in which one woman donates an egg to another woman whose infertility stems from dysfunction in ovulation. But childlessness can also be causcd by inability to sustain a pregnancy. Women suffering from this incapacity are often bedridden for weeks and even months to prevent spontaneous miscarriage, and the technology offers the option of another woman carrying the pregnancy of a child conceived from the childless woman's egg. Nothing rational is accomplished by naming the childless woman "egg donor" and subordinating her claim to legal parenthood to that of the carrying mother. The only perceivable objection to such reproductive relations is that they are too close to surrogate motherhood for comfort.

The technical separation of genetic and gestational motherhood makes it all the more imperative to address the crucial issue raised by surrogacy: the woman's moral agency and autonomy over her reproductive capacities within the context of her social relations of reproduction. Competing claims to social motherhood can also be resolved (and legal motherhood defined) in accord with the prior-to-conception intentions of the collaborating adults.

CHAPTER 7

Contracting to Become a Parent

---

*There is nothing more alluring to man than this freedom of
conscience, but there is nothing more tormenting either.*
—*Fyodor Dostoyevsky,* The Brothers Karamazov

Before proceeding to elaborate on a contractual scheme for reproductive relations—through a discussion of specific problems that might arise in the performance of a surrogacy contract—I wish to discuss three concepts that are central to my analysis of reproduction as a matter of social relations: reproductive agency, responsibility, and privacy.

Reproductive Agency

Reproduction, like all other human activities, takes place in a social context and can be conscious, rational, moral, and political. Reproductive "agency" denotes the human capacity, regardless of gender, to exercise reason and choice in making autonomous decisions and to bear responsibility for the consequences. Accordingly, normative significance would attach to biological reproductive functions through the medium of the intentions of the collaborating persons. We have seen, however, that whereas the legislative regulation of artificial insemination relations implicitly acknowledges the intention of the sperm donor to dissociate biological from social fatherhood, there is a reluctance to do so in the case of the surrogate mother. That the surrogate mother freely agrees to bear a child for another person does not apparently affect her right to keep the child after birth. Even though such change of mind may involve a breach of the initial agreement, her biological relation to the child is considered, in effect, to override any claim made by the other parties. The question is whether the disparate treatment of sperm donor and surrogate mother is justified.

The instinctive response is that whereas biological gender might not generally be material in determining individual merit and desert, when it comes to reproduction there is no avoiding the fact that the woman has the womb. The circumstances of the surrogate mother do appear to differ essentially from those of the sperm donor for she is involved in the process of reproduction continuously until the child's birth. It would seem further that pregnancy is an emotionally volatile condition and that some kind of instinctive maternal bonding to the fetus takes place in the process. It would be inhumane, therefore, to insist that the surrogate give up the child if it happens that against all her original good intentions she has become emotionally attached to the child.

This paternalistic refusal to force the surrogate mother to keep to her word denies the notion of female reproductive agency and reinforces the traditional perception of women as imprisoned in the subjectivity of their wombs. The benevolent protection of women from themselves places an indelible stamp of illegitimacy on the notion of a woman contracting to bear a child for another person. It implies that reproductive matters are not proper subjects for legal relations, reinforcing the public-private dichotomy that relegates women's reproductive activity to the shadow life of a male-dominated socioeconomic political order.

What prevents the surrogate mother from making a legally binding commitment toward the sponsoring parents? The only possible answer is: her biology. Her state of mind at the moment of agreement is not to be taken seriously because it is subject to change during the performance of her undertaking, due to the nature of pregnancy. The insinuation is that it is unreasonable to expect her to keep her promise because her faculty of reason is suspended by the emotional facets of her biological constituency.

Even though the pregnant woman appears to be physically possessed with a spirit not her own, she is an autonomous human being, no less in control of her human faculties than any other person. Without disregarding the physical incapacitation or emotional upheaval that she may experience in this unique womanly feat, she needs no more and no less excuse for her condition beyond those civilly accorded to any other human being in analogous creative situations. To deny this is to exclude women from full-fledged membership in human society. A woman pregnant with child is no less deserving of special treatment than an artist pregnant with inspiration. But her special condition in no way justifies the condescension that denies her autonomy as a human being.

The notion of female reproductive agency suggests an alternative perspective that perceives women as rational moral agents, competent to assess the emotional stakes of reproductive activity and to assume responsibility for its consequences, and frees us to examine the social construction of some self-evident truisms about our biological nature. Under the double standard of reproductive conduct, women normally rear the children they bear, and there has been little opportunity to explore the nonbiological aspects of the mother-fetus relationship. Certainly women have never been free to contemplate the significance of biological motherhood as such. The assumption that there is an instinctive mother-fetus attachment, regardless of the mother's intentions as to the child's rearing after birth, appears to be a matter of pure speculation at this point, given that women have been socially bound to take care of their children. Similarly, until fairly recently, the mother-infant relation was assumed to be a matter of natural instinct. One of the effects of feminist analysis has been to expose the oppressive cultural parameters of the traditional perception of that relation and to demystify social motherhood. The practice of surrogate motherhood could well initiate a discourse that will legitimate women as separate persons and demystify biological motherhood.

Moreover, the objection to commercial surrogacy, while tolerating altruistic engagements, smacks of the double standard of morally proper conduct. If a surrogacy for money arrangement is illegal, it should be noted, then a surrogate who performs her part in the agreement will have no legal remedy against a sponsoring parent who refuses to pay her as agreed. The rationale for the extension of the baby barter ban from the area of adoption—apart from the financial incentive that supposedly distorts the woman's decision-making process and renders her choice involuntary—is that it commercializes reproductive activity and "commodifies" human life. There is a tendency to overlook the considerable economic activity that accompanies the establishment of both biological and nonbiological parent-child relations, involving medical professionals, lawyers, and social workers, at the very least. Why is it that we balk precisely at paying women for their reproductive services? Is there anything special in the nature of childbearing that affects the volition of a woman negotiating the economic value of her reproductive labor, or is it merely that our moral sensibility is offended by the image of a rational woman controlling her bodily resources and selling her birth power?

Responsibility

The cool-headed, detached attitude that informs deliberate reproductive activity goes against the grain of a patriarchal ideology that conceives of domestic relations as an insulated haven of emotion and affection amid a cold, impersonal economic-political world.[1] The normative upshot of this private-public dichotomy is to extol values of love and altruism in personal relations, as opposed to the market forces of power and self-interest. At the same time, however, the cushioned private realm of woman is deprecated in relation to the abrasive public realm of man. This is the "pedestal-cage" in which woman is first captured, then protected, and finally respected to the extent that "man aspires to clothe in his own dignity whatever he conquers and possesses."[2] Woman is confined to the noble domestic destiny of wife and mother by virtue of her supposedly natural timidity and delicacy; and the very same nature renders her inferior as a moral creature, incompetent and unfit to participate in the public world.[3]

Women have not only suffered inferior legal status because of their biology but have also been considered incapable of attaining the highest levels of moral development. Carol Gilligan, however, suggests that women do not meet the standards of theories of moral maturity simply because these standards are based on studies of men, whereas women tend to exercise a different mode of moral reasoning and decision making.[4] The male point of view is that moral problems arise from competing rights and are resolved by a formal and abstract mode of thinking. If we bother to study women as moral agents in the process of making decisions, as Gilligan has done, we discover a different point of view—the female voice— according to which moral problems arise from conflicting responsibilities and are resolved by a contextual and narrative mode of thinking. Neither mode is the exclusive possession of one or the other biological sex; on the contrary, both modes interplay in each individual. They depict the very poles of the human tension that lies at the root of any moral problem—between attachment and separation, connection and individuation.

The male voice espouses an ethic of justice and fairness, based on the building blocks of rights and rules. This voice has inspired modern political theory and jurisprudence in Western culture. The elementary concept of right derives from an image of the natural state of human being, in which the solitary individual exists in inherent conflict with the social environment.[5] Tension is resolved by authoritative rules that are applied hierarchically, from the general to the particular, to impose order on the chaos and terror of the natural human condition.

The concept of right also reflects the vulnerability of the individual to the sheer force of numbers. It denotes a sphere of guarded individuality that checks and balances the power of organized social collaboration, embodying a defensive strategy in the form of a counterassertion of normative power within the political configuration of society. At the same time, however, it pits individual against individual, vesting the power of final dispute resolution with the state through its judicial organ, along the lines of divide and conquer. Thus the contextual nature of the human condition is abstracted into atomized individuals making exclusive claim to turf that is their own. Liberty is the right to be let alone—trespassers will be prosecuted.

The female mode of morality reflects a different view of the natural human condition, one of connectedness and interdependence. Perhaps it stems from the imagery of the umbilical cord and the fundamental fact that we all come into being in the womb, intrinsically related to another human being. Indeed, the primal human experience—one that colors all future instances of social interaction—is the dependence of the vulnerable infant on the adult caretaker. According to Nancy Chodorow, this social relation, rather than simple biological anatomy, accounts for sex differences. Because women are universally responsible for early child care, girls are parented by a person of the same gender and come to experience themselves as more continuous with and related to the external object-world than boys, who come to define themselves as more separate and distinct, with a greater sense of ego boundaries and differentiation. "The basic feminine sense of self is connected to the world, the basic masculine sense of self is separate."[6]

The male view of separate being posits what Gilligan calls "an ethic of fairness and justice." The idea of patriarchy attributes an epistemological value of objective truth and point-of-viewlessness to this voice. But the female view of connected being posits "an ethic of passion and care" to complement the male view and presents a whole balanced picture of being in relation to others (see table).

The concept of responsibility in the ethic of passion and care correlates to that of right in the ethic of justice and fairness. In our current normative system (which expresses the male voice) a concept of responsibility already exists as a derivative of right.[7] What I am suggesting here within an ethic of passion and care is that responsibility is a primary concept from which rights may derive. This normative concept draws from the perception that the human condition is essentially social, in that a person always exists within a network of relations. It is most apposite to an analysis of human reproduction, which is the origin of all existence and fundamentally social. In the simplest terms, some form of collaboration between persons (at least one male and one female) is a necessary condition of reproduction. The connection of woman and embryo/fetus, and then of parent and infant, moreover, is the primary experience of

	Justice Fairness	Passion Care
Morality	*Order* objective logical abstract active	*Idiosyncracy* subjective intuitive contextual responsive
Truth	*Objective* universal rational impartial detached impersonal absolute	*Subjective* particular instinctive empathetic self-reflective interpersonal contingent
Method	*Analytic* linear hierarchical goal-oriented	*Synthetic* spiral egalitarian process-oriented
Function	*Separation*	*Connection*

every human being and precedes all social interaction. The concept of right fails to take into account this human connectedness, which is elementary in all forms of social reproductive relations. Indeed, the language of rights appears to reach its limits in this context. In the abortion controversy, for example, it leads to a moral stalemate between the competing rights of two supposedly separate subjects (woman and fetus), whereas the reality is a oneness of woman-with-child.[8]

In the ethic of justice and fairness duty appears as the correlative of right, and interests are accounted for as grounds for asserting a right. When rights conflict, an impartial judge will resolve the matter by weighing and balancing the underlying interests. In the ethic of passion and care, interest is the correlative of responsibility, which focuses on the decision-making process of the person whose contemplated action may affect the interests of others. Whereas the theory of rights regards freedom as the liberty of unrestrained choice, the theory of responsibility goes beyond the mere possibility of choice to the manner in which it is exercised. Autonomy replaces liberty to denote the act of choosing responsibly, acknowledging the social context in which a choice is made and the decision maker's ability to affect others as much as self through any chosen action. A responsible decision maker considers the potential impact of the possible courses of action on the interests of others and the consequent repercussions on his or her own situation in relation to those others.[9]

Having said all this, I would define the primary normative concept of responsibility as the allocation of authority to decide on a course of action in accord with the agent's autonomous perception of the interests that the agent and others have in relation to the contemplated action. The norm that allocates the decision-making authority would determine the scope of the interpersonal situation in terms of the persons whose interests the agent must take into account and then vest the authority with one of the involved persons—indeed, with the one likely to be most fundamentally affected by the outcome of the decision. Once the agent has reached a decision, a norm is established that determines the relative prevalence of the various involved interests, or the particular rights of the involved persons. The agent would be presumed to have properly weighed the interests as a responsible person, and the validity of this decision could be challenged only by a person whose interest has been adversely affected, on the ground that, in the circumstances, such consequence is wholly unreasonable.

This scheme presents a nonhierarchical model for decentralized normative authority and idiosyncratic resolution of conflict. The norms that allocate the decision-making authority identify the agent in the context of the specific social situation. They have no substantive content but merely delineate the network of human relations within which personal interests arise and are to be taken into account. Beyond that, choice is made ad hoc, focusing on the nature of the circumstances. Legitimacy lies in respect for authority and not in the threat of force. Where the idea of right externalizes conflict to be resolved by an impartial umpire, the idea of responsibility internalizes the conflict in the self-reflective personality of the decision-making agent.

Privacy

If these two concepts of agency and responsibility are to be the governing principles in the law of reproduction, they must find an anchor in existing legal doctrine. I attempted above to show that contract can be used to implement these principles. But reproduction raises issues that are so fundamental as to be of constitutional importance, and on this level I suggest that personal interests should be protected as a mater of constitutional privacy.

The United States Constitution mentions neither reproduction nor the marital family. These matters were probably not thought to have political significance when this document was drafted—if the biological family was "natural" it would not merit attention in a document that dealt with the distribution of political power. The states thus retained jurisdiction over the body of family law that developed during the nineteenth century, along with the social changes in domestic relations and the legal position of women and children. But state regulation of the family reached its constitutional limitations at the beginning of the twentieth century, when the U.S. Supreme Court enunciated the principle that parental autonomy protected the child-rearing function from undue state intervention.[10]

Reproduction as such was first recognized as a subject of constitutional protection when a male offender challenged a state law imposing sterilization as a criminal sanction. The court held that the law violated a fundamental "right to procreate."[11] Then a statute prohibiting the use of contraceptives was struck down as violating a constitutionally guaranteed "zone of privacy" in marriage.[12] In *Roe v. Wade* (1973),[13] the Supreme Court subsequently held that the constitutional right to personal privacy embraced a woman's abortion decision. Although the Constitution did not explicitly mention this right, the court had recognized it in relation to certain fundamental personal rights in the areas of marriage, family relations, procreation, contraception, and child rearing and education, and it would now extend it to include a woman's decision to terminate a pregnancy.

Privacy in contraception and abortion protects a decision *not* to reproduce. The new reproductive technology involves positive decisions to reproduce, which should also be regarded as lying within the realm of privacy as a matter of personal decision-making authority. First, autonomy in reproductive decisions provides a check against the technical control of reproduction by detached parties for economic or political ends. Second, idiosyncracy and diversity in circumstances of birth guarantee the continuing enrichment of human experience. Third, given the novelty of the technological options and the general flux in social norms of family, the state should refrain at this point from imposing any one viewpoint as to the propriety of reproductive activity and allow norms to emerge case by case from the grass-roots level on the basis of experience.

Under current legal doctrine, privacy appears to consist in a right to be let alone. In the scheme proposed here, privacy denotes responsibility within a context of social relations for idiosyncratic decisions that are effectuated through contract. It contains two elements: the authority to make a decision, and the capacity to create an effective legal relationship with others to implement that decision. The meaningful exercise of private decision-making authority requires the state to acknowledge and enforce contractual relations that embody consensual reproductive collaboration. Privacy thus replaces norms of marriage and illegitimacy as a constitutional principle that defines legal parent-child relations in accord with autonomous contractual agreement. Any state-imposed restriction on access to reproductive technology beyond that of general contractual capacity[14] would be considered a ruling on parental eligibility that is an a priori violation of constitutional privacy (unless justified on independent grounds, such as reasonable criteria for distributing a scarce resource). In principle, there would be no more legitimate or illegitimate reproduction—certainly there would be no more illegitimate children.

A Surrogacy Contract: Breach and Remedies

If a surrogacy agreement, then, is a legally binding contract, how do these concepts work in the case of a breach? If a monetary obligation is not met, the remedy would clearly be a monetary award. But the breach of a personal undertaking will be more problematic, and the remedy will depend among other things on the stage at which it occurs: before conception, during pregnancy, and after delivery of the child.

Prior to Conception

I have suggested that conception be the crucial moment at which the terms of the reproductive collaboration are legally finalized. If there is no conception, there is no contract. Even if the failure to conceive is willful—for example, refusal to cooperate in the artificial insemination procedure—it would make no sense for the law to intervene. It would be unthinkable to force a person physically to go ahead with a reproductive project he or she had decided not to do and utterly irresponsible toward the child-to-be for conception to occur under such conflict. Until the moment of conception there should be complete freedom of choice, unrestrained even by potential liability for monetary damages.

Conduct of Pregnancy

Under the contractual approach proposed here the sponsoring couple assume legal parenthood and are attached with legal responsibility for the child-to-be from the moment of conception. That responsibility entails the authority to make decisions concerning the child's welfare. But during pregnancy the child-to-be is in the physical care and control of the surrogate mother. It is therefore safe to assume that conflicts will arise over performance between the parties to a reproductive services contract.

How will we deal, for example, with a situation in which a child is born with a birth defect that can be traced back to the surrogate's wrongful conduct during pregnancy? I have already suggested that such an occurrence should not alter the sponsoring couple's legal responsibility for the child, which depends neither on whim nor on the "supply" of a "perfect product," but is effective and binding from the moment of conception. But if a causal relation can be established between the surrogate's behavior and the specific birth defect, should we hold her liable to pay damages? This kind of hindsight view of causation is typical to the law of torts liability in general and informs the analysis of liability for the sale of a defective product in particular. But if the focus is on the ongoing social relations of the reproducing adults rather than on the child as an end product, we would be more concerned with terms of the agreement that provide for measures of prevention and control during the course of pregnancy. From this perspective, a key question arises over the extent to which the surrogate mother may be reasonably restrained in the exercise of her personal liberty.

If a surrogacy agreement is not viewed as a contract to produce an almost perfect child, then the sponsoring parents must be assumed to have taken the risk of imperfection, as in the case of ordinary sexual reproduction. Yet a science of prenatal medicine increasingly points to various measures for avoiding or reducing that risk, which necessarily involve the collaboration of the pregnant woman. Responsible sponsoring parents could be expected to inform themselves of the various possibilities of risk and incorporate appropriate provisions in the agreement. They could also be expected to take into account that the agreement will be unenforceable to the extent that it restrains the surrogate mother's personal liberty and violates her bodily integrity. Viewed from the perspective of the social relations of reproduction, the risk of imperfection inheres in the adults themselves. The surrogate mother is neither an incubator nor a machine that produces made-to-measure babies, and her independent personality entails limits on the ways in which she may be controlled. Indeed, respect for and sensibility to her particular personality may well be the key to her responsible performance of the contract. The irreducible biological fact is that the pregnant woman has ultimate control over the fate of the fetus in her womb. Therefore, any relationship that entails the voluntary exercise of her reproductive capacity as a service to another becomes at some point a matter of trust—or, conversely, one of uncertainty and risk.

A typical surrogacy agreement may provide for regulation of cigarette, alcohol, and drug consumption, as well as for medical supervision of pregnancy and childbirth. The surrogate would assume all the risks incidental to conception, pregnancy, and childbirth, while the sponsoring father takes responsibility for all children of the pregnancy, including those born with congenital abnormalities.[15]

Abortion

The generally unenforceable nature of contracts for personal services also covers the possibility of abortion by the surrogate. But even though she cannot be forced to continue the pregnancy, this would amount to breach of the contract. Needless to say, the remedy would depend on the circumstances.

Given proper counseling and screening before entering a surrogacy agreement, the surrogate mother will be unlikely to decide arbitrarily to terminate the pregnancy. Even in the usual case of an unplanned pregnancy, an abortion decision is not a frivolous matter. Moreover, since abortion becomes increasingly stressful and complicated both emotionally and physically with the progression of the pregnancy, self-interest would dictate an early decision. Statistics show that over 90 percent of abortions occur within the first trimester and over 50 percent within the first eight weeks of pregnancy. These data reflect the sense that most women have of developmental stages in fetal life that correspond to changes in their relationship or obligation to the fetus. A miscarriage that occurs in the first or second month of a pregnancy may barely be noticed, whereas a miscarriage in the fifth or sixth month becomes an occasion for mourning the loss of "someone."[16]

Surrogacy agreements currently provide for spontaneous miscarriage within the first four months of pregnancy.[17] The surrogate mother is entitled to reimbursement of all expenses incidental to the pregnancy and the miscarriage, and the parties' contractual relation is terminated. In the case of a willful abortion within the first four months, the surrogate would obviously not be entitled to reimbursement of expenses incurred in the abortion, and she might be expected to repay all monies that she received in connection with conception and the early stages of gestation. Arguably, the sponsoring couple would have no grounds for claiming emotional damages. It is highly improbable that the surrogate mother would willfully and one-sidedly terminate her pregnancy through abortion at a later stage unless her health is threatened. In that event, the sponsoring parents ought properly to cover all related expenses and remunerate her in some way for her personal services as in the case of a spontaneous miscarriage.

The most problematic situation arises where there are so-called fetal indications of abortion. The *Baby M* agreement stipulated that if the fetus were found to be physiologically abnormal, the surrogate agreed to undergo abortion on demand of the sponsoring father. If she refused, the father's contractual obligations would cease to be binding.[18]

Prenatal diagnosis of fetal abnormalities in the present state of the art produces results at an advanced stage of pregnancy, toward the end of the second trimester.[19] Two possible situations present themselves. The first is that on diagnosis the sponsoring parents decide that they wish to have the pregnancy carried to term and to care for the child after birth, but the surrogate undergoes abortion contrary to their wishes. This scenario is highly improbable, because a late second trimester abortion involves labor and vaginal delivery and there would appear to be no advantage to the surrogate in choosing to abort rather than to give birth to a live child. The second possibility is the converse one: the sponsoring parents wish to terminate the pregnancy but the surrogate refuses.

The question whether the surrogate is legally bound to abort the child under her agreement is often put in terms of her capacity to waive a constitutionally protected right. The approach suggested here, which views the surrogacy arrangement as a contract for personal services, presumes that in any event she cannot be legally forced either to undergo or to refrain from abortion. This takes into account the irreducible fact that the conscious personality of the pregnant woman as biological custodian of the fetus—regardless of the social relations of reproduction and any recognized interest of the sponsoring parents—is the primary condition for the fetus's evolution from a potential to an actual human being.[20] Nevertheless, her refusal to comply with the sponsoring parents' wishes might have legal consequences if, as I shall argue below, they have formal authority to make a decision in this respect. Thus, if the surrogate insists on birthing the child, the consequence could be that legal responsibility for the child reverts to her.

Let us assume that medical monitoring of the pregnancy has revealed an irreparable fetal disorder that poses no threat to the health of the surrogate herself. The constitutional question is which party to the arrangement has the authority or legal power to decide whether the pregnancy should be brought to term or terminated at once. If it is the surrogate, then any action she takes, whether in compliance with or in breach of the agreement, cannot be legally challenged. The sponsoring parents are left wholly at her mercy, so to speak, with no legally recognized rights under the agreement, until the third trimester of pregnancy, when the surrogate no longer has a constitutional right under *Roe v. Wade* to choose abortion unless the pregnancy poses a physical threat to her health.[21] If, on the other hand, the sponsoring parents have a legally recognized contractual interest, then even though the surrogate cannot be constrained to act in accordance with that interest, they might have grounds to challenge her decision or claim compensation. This would mean that their contractual position includes authority to make decisions regarding the continuation or termination of the surrogate pregnancy, commonly referred to as the right to privacy in abortion.

The latter approach departs from the general understanding that it is the pregnant woman's constitutional authority to make such decisions. In fact, however, a strict reading of *Roe v. Wade* reveals that, in striking down criminal law restrictions on abortion, the Supreme Court accorded constitutional protection to the decision-making authority of the pregnant woman's attending physician. The court stated: "The decision vindicates the right of the physician to administer medical treatment according to his professional judgment up to the points where important state interests provide compelling justifications for intervention. Up to those points, the abortion decision in all its aspects is inherently, and primarily, a medical decision, and basic responsibility for it must rest with the physician."[22]

The popular understanding of the decision, as well as the actual practice of first trimester abortion on demand of the pregnant woman, followed from the court's finding of a constitutional guarantee of personal privacy that was broad enough to encompass a woman's decision to terminate a pregnancy. The fundamental nature of this choice was explained in terms of both immediate pregnancy-related health concerns and long-term child-rearing responsibilities.[23]

Returning to the surrogacy situation in which a fetal disorder has been medically diagnosed, the physician clearly has expertise in gathering and interpreting the pertinent data, but this has little or no bearing on the normative question of who has the authority to decide or act on the basis of those data. I am arguing that as between the surrogate and the sponsors, the latter ought to have the legal authority to decide because, in accordance with their agreement, they will bear the long-term responsibility of caring for the child after birth.

The proposition is that the specific content of the right to privacy—that is, the allocation of decision-making authority—is to be determined by the particular attendant social relations. The *Roe v. Wade* ruling should be read within the context before the court, in which biological motherhood in general implies social responsibility for the child's care after birth, both as a normative matter and as a social, cultural, and historical reality. Women generally live under strong and often coercive pressures for and against childbearing. Many women choose abortion reluctantly in spite of the stigma in situations of desperation, recognizing realistically that they cannot assure their own and a dependent child's survival within the social and economic constraints of their lives. Given these conditions of human reproduction it is imperative that women have general authority to make an abortion decision.[24]

In the surrogacy situation, however, the social relations differ. The parties' express intention is to depart from the norm that automatically attaches social parenthood to the biological relation. The pregnant woman does not contemplate responsibility for the child after birth. The surrogate's constitutional privacy consists in her personal authority to make a reproductive decision that specifically anticipates the dissociation of biological from social motherhood, supplemented by her capacity to enter legally effective contractual relations that determine the allocation of the child-rearing responsibility, regardless of gender and biological connection. The sponsoring parents have similar authority to make reproductive decisions and effectuate them by means of contract.[25]

The surrogacy agreement is therefore an exercise of both parties' privacy in reproduction, which creates a legal parent-child relation before conception. Although actual social parenthood cannot vest in the sponsoring parents until the child has independent extrauterine existence, they still have a legal relation to the fetus that is embodied in their contractual relation with the surrogate mother.[26] The essence of this relation, its whole purpose, is their subsequent assumption of social and legal parenthood. Since an abortion decision will fundamentally affect the long-term designs of the sponsoring parents, rather than those of the surrogate, it is they who should have the authority to make such a decision, even if it cannot be effectuated technically. In a sense, the surrogate mother provides caretaking services, like those of a wet nurse or a neonatal intensive care unit, that the sponsoring parents cannot provide themselves. If the law insists on viewing her relation to the fetus in the same way as it views an ordinary pregnancy, her constitutional right to choose abortion amounts to a constitutional right to change her mind.[27]

But if the surrogate cannot be physically forced to comply with the sponsoring parents' abortion decision, what is the legal effect of their authority? In other words, what remedy do they have for the surrogate's breach? As suggested above, the consequence could be that legal parenthood for the child reverts to the surrogate mother— that is, she would reassume responsibility for the child's long-term care. The question would then arise whether the child's father would also be responsible, for example, to pay child support. According to the general rule, such support is the child's right and cannot be waived by her parent. It should be noted, accordingly, that even if the surrogate agrees not to claim child support, the agreement would not hold up in court.

It would seem that the father's responsibility toward the child is such that the surrogate's refusal to comply with his abortion decision does not completely release him from the obligations of legal parenthood, even if the terms of the initial contract are modified as a result. Responsibility for his reproductive activity means not only that he assumes a risk of imperfection in the child but also that he acknowledges the limits of his capacity to control the surrogate mother. The same would apply in the ordinary case of sexual reproduction, where the father wishes the pregnancy to be terminated and the mother does not. Although one might make a theoretical argument for the father's right to veto a pregnancy (claiming, for example, that no child should be brought into the world unless wanted by both parents), the biological reality is such that birth power is in the hands of the carrying mother.[28]

Fetal Therapy

So far the question of prenatal diagnosis has been discussed in terms of a choice between abortion and birth. Recent medical developments point to a third course of action: in utero fetal therapy. To what extent may a surrogate mother be expected to submit to such medical intervention? It is important to note that much of the therapy is at a preliminary, experimental stage. Of the many detectable fetal disorders only a few are amenable to treatment before birth, and some methods have not yet been proven effective.[29] An ethical question, however, presents itself—once fetal therapy has become standard practice—as to a pregnant woman's right to refuse treatment. Assuming "minimal risk" to the woman, it has been argued that the ethics of both the medical profession and responsible parenthood warrant administration of the treatment.[30] Whether any kind of surgical intervention for the sake of the fetus can be considered as posing minimal risk to the mother, is questionable, however. Whatever the ethical consideration, moreover, legal coercion may well be morally self-defeating in its violation of principles of bodily integrity and autonomy.[31]

The tendency of medical experts to speak on behalf of the fetus as an entity abstracted from the context of the pregnant woman's personality has led to a mode of discourse that opposes the woman's rights to those of the fetus. In the case of a "maternal-fetal conflict," it is argued that if the fetus is viable, the state has a compelling interest in its potential life under *Roe v. Wade,* and the woman loses the liberty to act in ways that would adversely affect it. She is considered to have waived her right to resist bodily intrusions for the sake of the fetus by choosing to bring the pregnancy to the stage of viability, and she may be required to submit to in utero therapy "essential" to the fetus's health so long as it does not pose "substantial" threats to her own health.[32] The logic of this argument is unclear. Does the fact that a woman chose not to abort mean that she waived her autonomy to make decisions regarding the conduct of her pregnancy? And who decides—and according to which criteria—what constitutes a substantial threat to her health? Surely it may be argued that any surgical intervention poses such a threat, except that ordinarily the benefits outweigh the risks for the patient (whereas here the fetus and not the woman benefits from the treatment).

To defer to medical authority on the correct management of pregnancy appears to be in tune with the view that a pregnant woman can be held liable in tort for prenatal injury to the fetus incurred in the negligent management of pregnancy,[33] as well as with policies that exclude women of childbearing age from workplaces that involve reproductive hazards.[34] In both cases spokespersons of medical science propose supposedly objective standards for evaluating reasonable or acceptable risk to the fetus, without much regard for the autonomy of the pregnant woman. To the extent that her interests differ from those asserted on behalf of the fetus, a "maternal-fetal conflict" exists.

An alternative approach regards the fetus and woman as interwoven, and the physician collaborates with the woman in a "maternal project" that leaves the power of decision in the hands of the woman, who is presumed to be committed to the welfare of the fetus. "The interests of fetus and woman are so intimately bound that one cannot speak of their distinct, let alone conflicting interests without simplifying distortion. Mother-and-child is a complex, both bodily and morally."[35] This approach recognizes the reality in which the woman-with-child is the primary agent of the fetus's potentiality and acknowledges her independent personality as well as her rational capacity to make responsible and informed reproductive decisions.

If a pregnant woman is accorded the respect due her as a responsible moral agent, then her reproductive decisions—including the "wrong" ones—should be treated with deference, except where a particular decision is unequivocally *un*reasonable. The upshot with respect to the surrogacy context is that the surrogate mother, as physical agent of the fetus's potentiality, retains a control over her gestational activity that must be accepted by the sponsoring parents. This is the irreducible special biological power of women. The sponsoring parents may legally challenge the surrogate's discretion in two cases only—breach of an express contractual undertaking, or wholly unreasonable conduct—and the most they can expect in terms of legal remedy is some form of compensatory relief. Otherwise they must carry the risk of human imperfection in reproduction.

Custody

In a sense, the greatest risk is that the surrogate mother will refuse to relinquish the child after birth. The question then is whether the legal system will force her to do so. On the face of it the rule that contracts for personal services are not specifically enforced would seem to apply. The general remedy for breach of contract is monetary. A decree of specific performance ordering the breaching party to do the very thing she agreed upon will be granted only if damages would be an inadequate remedy. Even then a court will not normally decree specific performance where ongoing court supervision is necessary for the order to be effective, as in a contract for personal services.[36]

The reluctance to order a surrogate mother to relinquish her child cannot, however, be entirely explained in this way. After all, she has performed the reproductive services that she contracted to provide. The reluctance of the court is to force her to separate from the child to which she has become emotionally attached. Analogous instances of contractual relations exist involving a personal and emotionally loaded duty of performance, such as a sculptor working on commission. It is, technically impossible to force the sculptor to create a piece of art, but once it is completed the sculptor cannot refuse to deliver it to the commissioning party merely because she or he wants to keep it. Similarly, it may be technically impossible to force a surrogate mother to conceive and carry a pregnancy to term, since these are personal services that depend ultimately on her continuing voluntary cooperation. But once the child has been born, why should her emotional involvement prevent the child's placement with the sponsoring parents?

The part of the surrogacy agreement that addresses the child's placement is akin to a custody agreement. Courts usually honor such agreements unless there has been a significant change in circumstances that justify modification of the agreement, having regard to the best interests of the child.[37] Assuming that both the surrogate mother and the sponsoring couple are more or less equally competent to care for the child, a commitment to freedom of contract would favor the sponsoring couple as custodians, whereas sympathy for the gestational bond between mother and child would favor the surrogate mother.

The biological relation as such appears to be immaterial. Both the surrogate and the sponsoring father typically have a biological interest in the child. But even if the sponsoring parent has no biological relation to the child—as, for example, where a single man or woman commissions the surrogate mother to conceive through artificial insemination with sperm from an anonymous donor—the contractual approach would favor the sponsoring party on the basis of the social relations of reproduction and the legitimate expectations that arise therefrom.[38] Likewise, even if the surrogate mother has no genetic relation to the child—as, for example, where she has carried the pregnancy of a child conceived from the egg of another woman—sympathy for the gestational bond would still favor her as custodian.

The perception of a mother-child gestational bond is not merely a matter of sympathy toward the mother. It also lays the ground for a best-interest-of-the-child argument. The in utero bonding of fetus with mother would seem to dictate that the child remain with the surrogate and to override the sponsoring parents' contractual claim. Thus, Britain's Warnock Committee stated that surrogate arrangements are, among other things, "potentially damaging to the child, whose bonds with the carrying mother, regardless of genetic connections, are held to be strong, and whose welfare must be considered of paramount importance." The psychological or emotional dimensions of fetal bonding are not, however, altogether clear. A dissenting minority on the committee pointed out that "as very little is actually known about the extent to which bonding occurs when the child is *in utero,* no great claims should be made in this respect."[39] Indeed, the generally accepted view of Goldstein, Freud, and Solnit is that a newborn child has no appreciation of biological relation as such and responds to any adult who provides for its needs and cares for its physical and emotional development.[40]

The contractual approach advocated here stems, among other things, from a critique of the idea that mothers bond instinctively with their children since this concept binds and confines women to a biological destiny and impedes their individuation as autonomous persons while excluding men from the role of social parent. Moreover, if responsibility—as opposed to right—is taken as the key concept in the regulation of interpersonal relations, then adult responsibility becomes the correlative of the interests of the child. From this point of view, a policy that renders a surrogacy agreement unenforceable in effect encourages the surrogate to act irresponsibly toward the other adults involved in the arrangement. If adult responsibility is the measure of the child's best interests, then one who demonstrates consistency in his or her initial commitment is surely more deserving of the title of legal parent.

Intimacy or Anonymity

The morality of surrogate mother arrangements depends largely on *how* they are carried out. In this respect, the experience of open adoption is highly pertinent.

A major concern about surrogacy is the potential commodification and commercialization of infant life. This is part of a broader concern about the dehumanization attendant to reproductive technology in general. In relation to surrogacy in particular, there may be concern that by giving legal effect to these arrangements we are adopting a "male" worldview that reduces human experience to its political and economic value. A woman's trading with her reproductive capacity may be seen as an assimilation of men's biological alienation from their offspring. It is fair to assume, though, that there would be little adherence to the view that behavioral irresponsibility of men as fathers is biologically determined, and there appears to be no reason to think that women will imitate such conduct.

The suggestion that a woman can be legally bound to a voluntary agreement to bear a child for another person implies nothing more than that she will have no *legal* rights or responsibilities toward the child. It does not necessarily mean that she will have no human contact with the child or ongoing interest in the child's welfare. But the models of adoption and artificial insemination are based on a principle of the parties' mutual anonymity, which prevents such contact. If the social relations of surrogacy are open, a different picture emerges. Aside from the possibility of ongoing contact between the surrogate and the child by according her visitation rights, the surrogate's initial undertaking appears to be more responsible where she is active in selecting the persons who will act as the child's social parents.

It will be recalled that the two main grounds for sperm donor anonymity are protection of the donor from a paternity action and protection of the integrity of the adoptive family. The first is redundant when the law is clear about the parties' legal rights and responsibilities. The second is pertinent to a scenario of closed adoption. The fear of the birth mother's ghostlike reappearance to harass the adoptive family could well be a guilt reaction to the radical consequences of closed adoption. Birth mothers may not be so much interested in reclaiming the mother-child relation as in having information about and some kind of access to the child. As for the child's emotional security, the appearance or presence of a nonlegal biological parent is more likely to be injurious if the child's origins are shrouded in mysterious secrecy like a skeleton in the family closet. Indeed, within the context of an increasing number of blended postdivorce families, the questions that the child may pose with respect to his or her relation to the surrogate mother (and her family) are not unique. The apparent threat that surrogacy poses to the family seems trivial compared to the rapid changes in the structure of the modern family.[41]

Another argument for openness and intimacy as opposed to secrecy and anonymity—made above in the adoption context—addresses the possible exploitation of the parties by a disinterested intermediary who controls the flow of information between them. It is not impossible to apply a policy of anonymity to the surrogacy situation in spite of the surrogate's continued physical presence and involvement in the reproductive process until the child's birth. At least one surrogacy agency has, in fact, developed an elaborate system of paperwork and intermediary activity to attain this end.[42] However, a surrogate mother (or sperm donor, for that matter)— ideally responsible and concerned for her offspring—can be allowed to decide for herself whether the candidate sponsoring parents satisfy her expectations and standards in terms of what she considers suitable conditions for raising a child. The sponsoring parents can also be allowed to make their own decision regarding the suitability of the surrogate in terms of general personality and capacity to act responsibly.

Where these decisions are left to a detached intermediary, the personalities of the involved parties tend to be quantified in the form of medical history records, financial statements, socioeconomic profiles, and the like. These may well be relevant or important, but those that resist quantification are equally so. What is more, the real dehumanizing threat of noncoital reproduction is that it allows the involvement of detached parties for economic or political ends that go beyond the unscrupulous operations of a small-town black market profiteer. Human life could indeed be turned into a mere commodity were a commercial enterprise to use reproductive technology to breed a cheap labor force or were a totalitarian state to implement a perverted political vision of socioeconomic stratification. It ought, therefore, be a constitutional matter for the individual to retain the utmost control over the initiation of reproduction and the choice of method, subject always to personal responsibility for the consequences of those decisions.

Contract is a legal instrument for the collaboration of autonomous individuals, and the rules of contract law typically develop case by case in accord with the actual experience of breakdown in such relations. Because we know so little about reproductive relations, constrained as we are within the limits of our experience of sexual reproduction, a contractual scheme would allow freedom to experiment and acquire knowledge. But the model of contract law is based on the idea of a free market in which interests are traded on the assumption of equally distributed bargaining power. The pure form does not exist in reality, since neither individual freedom nor equality can be extricated from the constraints of social existence. The practice of surrogacy has already shown some patterns of breakdown in relations that are indicative of the relative strengths and weaknesses of the bargaining parties. Certain safeguards can be established on the basis of this experience without unduly restricting the parties' autonomy.

It might be wise, for example, to restrict surrogate mother activity to women above the age of legal maturity who have already experienced childbirth, to insure that they appreciate the nature of their undertaking. Professional counseling to both parties could be mandated as a prerequisite to court approval of the agreement before it is effectuated by conception. Reasonable fees for the services of intermediaries could also be regulated in this fashion.

As it is now, at least under the *Baby M* ruling, the sponsoring parents have no legal protection of their interests. Not only does the surrogate mother retain physical control over the pregnancy, but she has a legal right to obstruct implementation of the agreement. Since there is no legal recognition of the peculiar relation of the sponsoring parents to the child until the ordinary procedure of postnatal adoption is effected, the method by which they protect themselves against the possibility of the surrogate withholding her consent is to withhold payment of the surrogate fee. As a result, the surrogacy agreement indeed takes on the semblance of a contract for the sale of a child. If the binding effect of the parties' agreement on the sponsoring couple's parental status is recognized from the beginning through a procedure of court approval, there would be no reason to defer payment of the surrogate fee. Indeed to do so renders the surrogate mother particularly vulnerable vis-à-vis the sponsoring parents. The power that she necessarily and inherently retains over the fetus should not be taken into consideration as a matter of legitimate bargaining power, since the child-to-be should always be treated as the end of the parties' relationship rather than a means. Payment of the fee in installments up until the birth of the child would equalize the relations of the parties and reflect more accurately the nature of their transaction for the sale of reproductive services.

The susceptibility of the surrogate mother to exploitation by the sponsoring parents is a grave concern that arises in light of the typical socioeconomic disparity of the contracting parties and the cultural tendency to abstract the fetus from the pregnant woman and to regard her as a mere physical support system. Thus, for example, the *Baby M* agreement stipulated that in the event of a stillbirth, the surrogate mother would receive only a small fraction of the compensation she was entitled to in the case of a healthy newborn. This is a prime example of the objectification of the surrogate mother and the commodification of the child. The surrogate cannot guarantee a perfect baby, and the sponsoring parents must not only accept the risk of human imperfection but also remunerate the surrogate for her actual services, regardless of the end-product.

Arguably, a model of open relations in which the sponsoring parents have firsthand knowledge of the surrogate's concrete personality would ameliorate this propensity. We have seen that the cultural nonentity of the pregnant woman is still very much evident in attitudes that inform the administration of the most sophisticated techniques of infertility therapy. If this is to change reproductive consciousness must be transformed so as to recognize the reproducing woman as an autonomous moral and economic agent. But this contractual scheme implies a free market in reproduction, which challenges and undermines the inferior economic existence of women under patriarchy and the various ideological mechanisms that exclude them from full participation in the public world of male power.

CHAPTER 8

Woman as Economic Being

Girls who can stand in a line and look pretty are as
numerous as labourers who can swing a pick.
—*Theodore Dreiser,* Sister Carrie

Reproductive Technology:
Liberation or Manipulation?

We have seen that objection to surrogacy relations generally turns
on the extension of reproductive relations beyond the officially exclusive sphere of marriage, the denial of the mother-child gestational
bond, and the insinuation of baby trafficking activity. To the extent
that feminist literature directly addresses the question of surrogacy,
its critical concerns are the alienation of women from their reproductive activity by medical technology and their objectification and
susceptibility to economic exploitation as human breeders. Within
the general context of the growing control of reproduction by a male-
dominated medical profession,[1] surrogacy appears to be an additional means to perpetuate the patriarchal definition of woman according to a function that reduces her to a "mother machine."

The feminist response to the new technology has, however, not
been consistent. In 1970 Shulamith Firestone claimed that "artificial" reproduction was not inherently dehumanizing and hailed a
technology that, if used properly, could free women and the entire
human species from the tyranny of biological destiny. Writing when
the subject of reproduction was still taboo and when women who
came out against motherhood were labeled "neurotic, unable, child-
hating and therefore 'unfit,' " she dismissed the current feminist cult
of natural childbirth as reactionary. "Pregnancy is barbaric," she
stated bluntly, ". . . the temporary deformation of the body of the
individual for the sake of the species. Moreover, childbirth *hurts*
. . . like shitting a pumpkin."[2]

The possibility of choice for women as regards biological motherhood, Firestone argued, would redistribute the emotional, psychological, and physical costs of reproduction and correct the tragic cultural sacrifice of women that was a consequence of the division of the psyche into male and female. The option of artificial reproduction would permit an honest reexamination of the value of motherhood. The confinement of women within the role of mother and the taboo of those who chose not to fill that role would persist until having children by artificial means was as legitimate as traditional childbearing. Firestone seemed to envision a revolution that would transcend the gender boundaries of biological reproduction and bring about an androgynous culture of parenthood in which men could choose to become fathers as much as women could choose not to become mothers.

Juliet Mitchell, however, claimed that this was a simplistic vision that ignored the history of the economic oppression of women as a class under capitalism. Biology, or physical deficiency, did not adequately explain women's relegation to inferior status. Nor could a technology that transcended biology be properly discussed without paying attention to the total economic political structure in which it was employed. Nevertheless, technology had the potential to change "the mode of reproduction" that had been defined so far by its uncontrollable, natural character as a matter of unmodified biological fact. As long as reproduction remained a natural phenomenon, women were effectively doomed to social exploitation. Women could not be "masters" of their lives so long as their social existence remained subject to biological processes outside their control. Technical possibilities now existed to transform and humanize the most natural part of human culture.[3]

In a more emotive vein, Adrienne Rich, too, considered the social limitations to realization of the technological potential. The "institution of motherhood" prescribed by patriarchal culture demands of women maternal instinct rather than intelligence, selflessness rather than self-realization, relation to others rather than the creation of self. Under ideal conditions, perhaps made possible by the technology, women would choose not only whether, when, and where to bear children but also the method of reproduction as a free and intelligent undertaking. But this idea could not be realized without examining "the shadow-images we carry out of the magical thinking of Eve's curse and the social victimization of women-as-mothers."[4]

In light of the experience gained from the growth in available technological options, latter-day feminists point out the powerlessness of women and their continued subjection to old oppressive attitudes. Women remain the targets of manipulation and lack control over their reproductive activity both at the professional level as scientists or doctors and at the personal level as consumers. "At the mercy of 'benevolent' male experts. At the mercy of technologies developed by men who see women as something 'other', 'strange', 'not-the-norm'. Technologies that were not made by us. We doubt that they are in women's interests."[5]

The scientific control of reproduction seems in many ways merely to provide highly efficient means to reinforce the patriarchal subjugation of women as objects for sex and reproduction. Andrea Dworkin describes two models that essentially determine the social control of women under patriarchy: the brothel model and the farming model. "The brothel model relates to prostitution, narrowly defined; women collected together for the purposes of sex with men; women whose function is explicitly non-reproductive. . . . The farming model relates to motherhood, women as a class planted with the male seed and harvested."[6]

Under the farming model women are appropriated through marriage by individual men to produce their offspring. Because a man's property reflects his station in life, and because marriage involves a continuing personal relationship, the man has a stake in the welfare of his woman. Indeed, "to husband" means "to manage thriftly . . . to till and cultivate."[7] However, the control of reproduction through the subjection of women has not been efficient since the quantity and quality of the "crop" depend largely on uncontrollable factors outside the realm of the social husband-wife relation. Changes in reproductive technology replace the husband's individual social control with the much more precise medical control of reproducing women as a group, approximating the efficiency of the brothel model.

Artificial insemination, in vitro fertilization, sex selection, genetic engineering, fetal monitoring, artificial wombs that keep the fetus alive outside the mother's body, fetal surgery, embryo transplants, and eventual cloning . . . all these reproductive intrusions make the womb the province of the doctor, not the woman; all make the womb extractable from the woman as a whole person in the same way the vagina (or sex) is now; some make the womb extraneous altogether or eventually extraneous; all make reproduction controllable by men on a scale heretofore unimaginable.[8]

Given these cultural parameters and the long-standing tradition of women's exploitation and victimization under the brothel model, Dworkin argues that surrogacy amounts to nothing less than a new-wave form of prostitution. Where the state has constructed the social, economic, and political situation in which the sale of some sexual or reproductive capacity is necessary to the survival of women it is meaningless to speak of the "free will" of the surrogate mother.[9] Indeed, even though for years feminists took the position that it was wrong to tell women what they could or could not do with their bodies, a brief filed by a group of feminists in the *Baby M* case argued that legalization of surrogacy would lead to the exploitation of poor women by more affluent childless couples and reduce the surrogate mother to a mere commodity in the reproductive marketplace.[10]

The Social Construction of Will

The argument that the psychological constraints of patriarchy limit women's autonomy poses a serious challenge to the idea of a contractual scheme to regulate social reproductive relations. I have pointed out how women consented to participate in reproductive research without appreciating its experimental nature. Gena Corea suggests further that the very notion of a woman's informed consent to novel reproductive procedures is a "myth of voluntarism," considering the attitude that women are nothing unless they bear children and that they lose their basic identity if they are infertile. "When pharmacrats, and in some cases, husbands, speak to the unconscious of infertile women, playing on a fear of barrenness, which may signify to the woman abandonment, loss of love, they are exercising . . . an alternative kind of coercion. Coercion through the manipulation of the unconscious can operate without the person's knowledge that she is being coerced, without her resentment, and with the appearance of her consent."[11]

Judith Lorber suggests that advanced techniques of medical reproduction are being used primarily to normalize traditionally structured, upper-middle-class, two-parent (one male, one female) families. Instead of seeking psychosocial responses to cultural pressure so as to legitimate childlessness, the technology provides a physiological solution for childless married couples that fits them into the cultural norm. It might well be, moreover, that genetic continuity is more significant to men, for whom until now parenting has meant the passing on of one's genes, than to women, for whom parenting means bringing up a child. Thus, there appears to be a shift toward using in vitro fertilization to overcome male reproductive malfunctioning—although the women concerned were fertile and probably could have conceived with donor sperm through artificial insemination, they were willing to undergo for the benefit of their spouses a far more intrusive and manipulative procedure.[12]

The social construction of the childless woman's psychology, however, has no direct bearing on that of the surrogate mother. The feminist case against surrogacy rests rather on the objectification of female reproductive activity, the general devaluation of women's labor, and women's special vulnerability to economic exploitation within a patriarchal capitalist system. The individual woman and her will are mere fictions, it is argued, so long as she is engaged in those activities that define women as a class. Issues of female sexual and reproductive destiny cannot be resolved by individuals as individuals. To speak of individuality is merely to perpetuate the patriarchal capitalist system that sets the conditions for women's exploitation as a class.[13]

The author of a journalistic account of her experience in applying to be a candidate for surrogate motherhood concluded that it was consistent with a prostitution model.

> The surrogate is paid 'for giving the man what his wife can't.' She 'loves being pregnant,' and is valued solely and temporarily for her reproductive capacity. After 'she enters the fold' she is removed from standard legal protections and is subject to a variety of abuses. She is generally considered to be mercenary, collecting large unearned fees for her services, but the terms of the system are in reality such that she may lose more permanent opportunities for employment, and may end up injured or dead with no compensation at all. Even the glowing descriptions of the surrogates sound remarkably like a happy hooker with a heart of gold.[14]

Within this system, women are again divided along the lines of madonna-whore, and the infertile wife of the upper-class man becomes an accomplice to the exploitation of the lower-class woman. The continuing cultural pressure on women to realize themselves as mothers might well be a factor in the single-minded compulsion with which many childless couples pursue all available means to establish a family, including shady international adoptions, believing that money can buy everything. This should certainly be taken into account when considering the possible exploitation of surrogate mothers.

Beyond the socioeconomic disparity of the consumers of the medical technology and the women who are likely to offer their reproductive services for sale, moreover, the demographic profile of the consumers (affluent white married couples)[15] raises serious concern about racist undertones to an industry that responds to a shortage of adoptable (read "Caucasian") babies. In particular, the technical possibility of implanting a fertilized egg in the womb of a carrying mother has the horrifying potential of expanding into an international commerce in human reproduction, using and exploiting women from underdeveloped countries.[16]

Victims and Agents

Fears about the potential exploitation of women—well-founded though they may be—do not necessarily lead to the conclusion that surrogacy relations ought to be prohibited. The feminist opposition to surrogacy can be better understood within the context of two broader debates, the one concerning protectionist labor legislation and the other concerning pornography and female sexuality.

The debate over protectionist labor legislation goes back to the turn of the twentieth century, when there was a concerted attempt to redress the inequality in bargaining power of workers (men, women, and children) by regulating minimum standards of working conditions. Included among the protective measures were laws that excluded women workers from certain jobs altogether. The organized feminist movement had originally argued that women were entitled to the same human rights as men. But there had emerged by the beginning of the century an ideological claim to a special privilege for motherhood, based on values attributed to women's sphere in the home (compassion, nurturance, and morality), which supposedly rendered them unfit for competitive economic struggle. This translated into a professed public concern for the health and morals of the mothers of succeeding generations, and it became a major justification for limiting women's contractual right to negotiate the terms of their working conditions.[17]

In the case of *Lochner v. New York* in 1905, for example, the U.S. Supreme Court struck down a state law that limited the hours bakers could be required to work on grounds that it unduly interfered with the workers' and employers' right to freedom of contract.[18] But just three years later, in *Muller v. Oregon,* the court upheld a statute imposing limitations on the hours that women would be permitted to work in factories, mechanical establishments, and laundries. The state referred to women's role as mothers and their relatively weak physical constitution in explaining the restriction of their freedom of contract as workers. The Supreme Court indeed justified disparate treatment of men and women on these grounds: "That woman's physical structure and the performance of the maternal functions place her at a disadvantage in the struggle for subsistence is obvious. This is especially true when the burdens of motherhood are upon her. . . . [A]s healthy mothers are essential to vigorous offspring, the physical well-being of women becomes an object of public interest and care in order to preserve the strength and vigor of the race."[19]

As a consequence, women were not free to bargain for larger salaries by giving up their shorter hours. Likewise, they were excluded from many jobs that required overtime work and commanded appropriately higher wages.[20] In a way, then, the protective measures that accorded women special treatment became a key mechanism for perpetuating their inferior economic station. While women's participation in the workforce increased, the law attempted to avoid changes in their social roles that more freely available economic opportunities might have permitted. By denying women the opportunity to work as full-fledged equal wage earners, the protective legislation institutionalized reproduction as women's primary social role.[21]

The debate over the propriety of special treatment for women took place in the frame of a traditional legal approach to discrimination that generally propounded an assimilationist Aristotelian concept of equal treatment for equally situated persons. To the extent that women were equally situated to men they would receive equal treatment, but "real" differences between women and men would justify disparate treatment. In *Geduldig v. Aiello* (1974), for example, the Supreme Court applied this approach to conclude that the exclusion of pregnancy-related disabilities from coverage under an otherwise comprehensive state disability insurance program was justified, reasoning that the program did not exclude anyone from eligibility because of gender but merely removed one physical condition—pregnancy—from the list of compensable disabilities.[22]

This decision illustrates the tendency to confuse biological and socially constructed stereotypical differences in defining what constitutes "real" difference, which is most problematic with respect to reproductive roles. Legal norms based on assumptions about universal sex-based difference tend to create obstacles for the individual woman who wishes to deviate from traditionally prescribed social roles. Moreover, the Aristotelian view regards inequality as an aberration from the norm of equality between individuals and ignores the fact that male supremacy is a complete social system for the advantage of one sex over another. Thus Catharine MacKinnon contrasted this "differences approach" to the "inequality approach," according to which the test for gender discrimination would be "whether the policy or practice in question integrally contributes to the maintenance of an underclass or a deprived position because of gender status."[23]

The current trend among so-called liberal feminist thinkers appears to be the attempt to transcend socially defined sex-based constraints and to acknowledge the individual woman's right to self-definition, without denying the social parameters of women's oppression as a class and without ignoring the categorical sex difference that most women but no men possess the capacity to bear children. The proper question according to this approach is: How can we accommodate those differences relevant for legal purposes without perpetuating the inferior status of women as a class?[24] The challenge is to reconcile the concepts of equality and difference without falling into the trap of paternalist protectionism. A simple analysis of economic or political egalitarianism, assuming the sameness of men and women, is clearly inadequate. But this does not mean that the human qualities common to men and women are less important than the differences between them. It means rather that sexual particularity must be taken into account.[25]

The tension between treating women as a disadvantaged group of victims and as individual autonomous agents is conspicuous in the current feminist debate over the nature of female sexuality, which has centered on antipornography activism. On one side there is the position, advocated most forcefully by MacKinnon, that sexuality is a social sphere of male power of which forced sex is paradigmatic and that pornography merely reinforces the idea of male domination and female submission.

Women are socialized to passive receptivity; may have or perceive no alternative to acquiescence; may prefer it to the escalated risk of injury and the humiliation of a lost fight; submit to survive. . . . [M]ale initiatives toward women carry the fear of rape as support for persuading compliance, the resulting appearance of which has been called consent. Here the victim's perspective grasps what liberalism applied to women denies: that forced sex as sexuality is not exceptional in relations between the sexes but constitutes the social meaning of gender.[26]

Given the paradigm of forced sex, the very notion of women's free consent to heterosexual intercourse is called into question. Pornography, which portrays women submitting to various forms of sexual violation and abuse, ought not therefore to be protected under the constitution as free speech. "It eroticizes hierarchy, it sexualizes inequality. It makes dominance and submission sex. Inequality is its central dynamic; the illusion of freedom coming together with the reality of force is central to its working."[27]

On the other side of the sexuality debate, however, is a position premised on the faculty of intrinsic human agency that argues for the individual woman's right to expose herself to risk and danger in sexual relations. Where the view of women as victims of forced sex appears to imply the need to boycott heterosexual intercourse in order to create neutral conditions for a true redefinition of female sexuality, the view of women as free agents implies that a reformulation of human sexuality leading to an enlightened humanity will best be accomplished through grass-roots explorations in the interaction of individuals.

Beyond the issue of free speech, the antipornography stance is problematic from this point of view on two principal counts. First, the substance of the arguments against pornography has much appeal for traditional sexual conservatives, implying a prescription of "politically correct" sexual conduct.[28] In doing so, it polarizes male and female sexuality, demonizing the former and idealizing the latter, and seems to imply a new biological reductionism that attributes the hierarchy of patriarchal gender relations to the rapaciousness of male biology.[29] Second, and more pertinent to the issue of female reproductive agency, the portrayal of women as members of a group that is culturally determined to be victimized amounts to a denial of the individual woman's faculty of self-determination and ignores the ways in which women can mold and take responsibility for their own lives. Thus Carole Vance asks: "Can women be sexual actors? Can we act on our own behalf? Or are we purely victims, whose efforts must be directed at resisting male depredations in a patriarchal culture?"[30]

Wages for Reproduction

The proposition of female agency in reproductive activity is analogous to that of sexual agency. The contractual scheme for reproductive relations that I propose is part of a feminism that supports women's experiments and encourages the acquisition of knowledge through individual experience. It insists that to overcome the psychological constraints of patriarchy women must regard themselves as subjects, actors, and agents of their individual sexual and reproductive activity.[31]

The idea of a free market in reproductive activity nevertheless contains a commercial element that could lead to what Linda Gordon called "a loss of mothering in a symbolic sense." The fear is of a completely individualized society in which all services are based on egoistic cash nexus relations without any forms from which children can learn about lasting nurturing human commitments. The problem is to reconcile a philosophy of personal agency with notions of constructive bonds between individuals.[32]

Although we do not want to sacrifice the value of altruism altogether for the sake of individuality, it is important to note the pathological aspects of the image of the nurturing woman. As much as women are connected with others, and particularly with their children, they also have difficulty with separation and individuation. Moreover, both Dorothy Dinnerstein and Nancy Chodorow have pointed out that the jealous proprietary monopoly of biological mothers over the rearing of infant children plays an active part in perpetuating sex-role differentiation.[33]

Although an economic analysis of reproduction uses a language that seems to reduce complex social relations to simplistic cold terms of commerce, or trade in commodities—a danger that must be duly apprehended—it brings to light a fact largely glossed over by patriarchal culture, that women's reproductive activity does have economic value. Indeed, the tendency to commodification is far greater when we focus on the child as "product" than when we focus on the birth mother as "producer."

It must be clear from the outset that the transaction under consideration is not for the sale of a baby but for the sale of reproductive services. Reproductive contracts are transactions in which custody of a child is transferred from one person to another, whereas the sale of a baby implies the transferral of property rights in a human being as a variation on slavery. The concept of custody does indeed contain an element of exclusive possession and control of the child. Certainly, property notions of exclusive ownership of women and their children form the historical source of our current law of parent-child relations. (Although contemporary family arrangements, specifically in open adoption or postdivorce situations involving visitation or even shared custody, indicate a relaxation in the possessive character of the exclusive parent-child relation.) There is, however, a difference between acquiring a position to exercise custodial control of a child and its abuse. A free market in reproduction—based on prior-to-conception agreements—does not involve the purchase of transferable rights or imply a right to resell a child. Rather, a childless couple is regarded as purchasing the reproductive labor of a birth mother so as to acquire the privilege of being responsible for the long-term care of a child. Once that responsibility is established, it cannot be relinquished except through the mechanism of statutory adoption.

The value of the reproductive services is determined by various factors of supply and demand. It may be reasonable to assume initially that remuneration for reproductive labor would be relatively low, as in the case of other transactions involving widely available bodily functions that require little training or expertise, such as manual labor. At the same time, the value of the personal services would reflect the costs directly related to pregnancy and childbirth, the costs of other economic opportunities the birth mother may forego while engaged in the reproductive project, and the emotional costs she may incur in giving birth to a child she will not keep. On the other side, the consumer demand would take into account the emotional costs of childlessness, the availability of adoptable newborns, and the economic costs of alternative forms of collaborative reproduction (for example, in vitro fertilization as compared to artificial insemination or open adoption). In addition, there are information costs involved in locating the parties and bringing them to a mutually satisfactory arrangement, having regard to individual preferences and tastes.[34]

Assuming an unsatisfied demand of childless couples, any legal restriction on permissible forms of reproductive collaboration would merely drive the activity underground, creating a black market. The risk of incurring criminal sanctions and the additional information costs of a clandestine market would result in artificially high prices. Moreover, intermediary exploitation and dishonesty is granted effective immunity where the activity is illegal, since the parties lack access to courts of law to enforce the terms of their transaction.[35] Beyond this, it appears generally that any policy prohibiting (rather than regulating) commercial activity in a given area of social interaction is premised ultimately on a denial of individual autonomy. As in the case of the war on drugs, the mentality of prohibition appears to treat people as objects to be controlled rather than as responsible actors. It is assumed that their behavior is not generated by an internalized value structure but by external forces. It follows that the individual's attempt to govern his or her own consciousness must be suppressed for fear of what that person may do or experience. The idea of individual responsibility or accountability is alien to this point of view.[36]

A free market would allow a new source of productive activity for women who presently have limited income-earning opportunities, with two positive distributive effects: a shift of wealth from the childless consumers to the presumably less advantaged reproducers, and a reallocation of economic returns away from the exploiting intermediaries to the birth mothers.

In spite of all this, the prospect of a market for reproductive services is disquieting, if not grotesque. We have an intuitive reaction that there is something fundamentally indecent in the possibility of prices, advertising, credit, discounts, and like attributes of consumer transactions.[37] It is not improbable, for example, that price differences would reflect racist prejudices that we strive particularly hard to overcome through other social policies.[38] And there is concern that a free market scheme would relegate underprivileged women to a new oppressed and undignified occupation, like prostitutes and wet nurses. But it should be obvious that the idea of a free market in reproduction does not attempt as such to rectify existing social inequities, and legal regulation could conceivably provide certain protections, such as court approval of reproductive agreements and minimum wage legislation.

There is, of course, the further objection that even if we call the transaction a contract for reproductive services rather than for the sale of a baby, the result is still the same—to put a monetary value on a life that is considered priceless. Yet the problem of pricing life is confronted in many areas of social activity, such as torts law, motor vehicle design, medical research, and most of all military strategics. Indeed, a similar debate took place in the late nineteenth century with respect to life insurance, which was thought to represent a form of trafficking in human lives.[39] Our acceptance of these instances of pricing life and death appears to be part of a complex process of transition in the cultural values of a postindustrial society. This process seems now to have reached the boundaries of the sacred institution of sexual-reproductive relations: marriage.

"What is it about child-bearing that makes it somehow dishonorable when done for money but most honorable when done for other reasons? Why does paying for childbirth or engaging in child-bearing for the sake of money convert a dignified activity into a despised one?"[40] Furthermore, why do we not object to paying doctors for their services in collaborative reproduction? Is the notion of paying for human life distasteful only when the recipient is the mother?

The idea of wages for reproduction poses an essential challenge to the public-private/market-family division that is the patriarchal foundation of our postindustrial economy. Woman as conscious, moral, social, and political being is also woman as economic being. We cannot separate ourselves from our economic existence or ignore the value (as commonplace as it may be) of our reproductive powers. The attachment of monetary value need not in itself determine the manner in which we conduct ourselves in our reproductive relations. But the failure to acknowledge the economic value of female reproductive labor is blind folly for those who wish for equity in women's social situation.

The Public-Private Dichotomy

The public-private division refers to two distinct matters: the dichotomy between the state and the economy (or civil society), as in the distinction between public and private law; and the dichotomy between the sphere of government and/or the marketplace and the family.[41] In feminist analysis, the public-private dichotomy generally denotes the ideological separation of the domestic and public aspects of social organization along lines of gender. In a patriarchal system women and their children find their primary social location in domestic relationships, assumed to be both natural and biological, whereas men find their primary social location in political and economic relations. The public sphere is considered to embody a "second" human nature, by which humanity transcends biological necessity to change and develop the history of the species in terms of nondomestic social organization.[42]

The ideological implication of male supremacy and female inferiority was mitigated by expounding the moral virtue of motherhood and glorifying the familial home as a haven conserving traditional values in face of modern industrial progress. Indeed, the "privatization" of the family was directly related to the industrial revolution, which separated the economic function of the household from that of commodity production by organized wage labor.[43] Whereas, under modern liberal theory, the marketplace came to be regarded as an area of self-interested activity governed by an individualistic ethic, the family came to be seen as an area of sharing, self-sacrifice, and cooperation, superseding the egoistic goals of its individual members under an altruistic ethic.[44]

The public-private dichotomy embodied a separate-but-equal worldview. In Dworkin's words: "The sphere of the woman was the home; the sphere of the man was the world. These were separate-but-equal domains. The woman was supposed to bear and raise the children; the man was supposed to impregnate her and support them. These were separate-but-equal duties. The woman had female capacities—she was intuitive, emotional, tender, charming. . . . The man had male capacities—he was logical, reasoning, strong, powerful. . . . These were separate-but-equal capacities. The woman was supposed to do domestic labor, the precise nature of which was determined by the husband's social class. The man was supposed to labor in the world for money, power, recognition, according to his social class. This was separate-but-equal labor."[45]

The separate-but-equal theory was accompanied by a seemingly neutral juridical approach of nonintervention in the private sphere, which in fact ratified and reinforced openly hierarchical social roles within the family. During the first half of the nineteenth century, a woman's subjection to her husband's control was a matter of law and custom. A married man and woman could not enter enforceable contracts with each other. The state refused to give legal effect to any attempt to define the rights and duties of spouses. Within the private family, there was a "state of nature" in which legal protection of one member from the harmful acts of another was unavailable. Until the mid-century passage of married women's property acts, whatever property or earnings women received belonged to their husbands. Men were free to decide how much support to provide their wives and children beyond a bare subsistence level.[46]

The latter-day feminist slogan, "The personal is the political" attempts to illuminate the reality of gender power relations that is obscured by the privatization of domestic life and to expose the collective nature of women's experience in the isolation of their homes. From this perspective, as MacKinnon points out, the doctrine of constitutional privacy seems to be one more facet of the law's hands-

off attitude to domestic relations that serves as a means to subordi-
nate women's collective needs to the imperatives of male supremacy.

> The very place (home, body), relations (sexual), activities (in-
> tercourse and reproduction), and feelings (intimacy, selfhood)
> that feminism finds central to women's subjection form the core
> of privacy doctrine. But when women are segregated in private,
> one at a time, a law of privacy will tend to protect the right of
> men 'to be let alone', to oppress us one at a time. . . . The
> private sphere, which confines and separates us, is therefore a
> political sphere, a common ground of our shared inequality. In
> feminist translation, the private is a sphere of battery, rape and
> women's exploited labor; of the central institutions whereby
> women are deprived of (as men are granted) identity, autonomy,
> control and self-determination; and of the primary activity
> through which male supremacy is expressed and enforced.[47]

Defining the domestic as women's proper sphere not only ex-
cludes women from the market and prescribes their economic dependence on men but also ignores the reality of the lives of many
women whom economic circumstances forces to seek their own
wage-earning opportunities. I have described how protectionist labor
legislation limited these opportunities by reference to women's role
as mothers. But women's contemporary economic situation also results from two concrete effects of the public-private division of labor: the segregation of the market place in terms of traditionally
male/traditionally female job classifications, and the systemic undervaluation of female labor.

The pattern of occupational segregation and its associated salary
inequities are well documented. Recent "comparable worth" studies
indicate that wage disparities between male- and female-dominated
occupations are only partly explained by job characteristics. Objective job-evaluation analyses based on such factors as skill, effort,
responsibility, and working conditions indicate that much of the
wage gap is due to the systemic underevaluation of women's work.[48]

Studies carried out primarily in the public sector have reported
consistently that female-dominated jobs command salaries 15 to 20

percent lower than comparable male-dominated jobs. Two specific examples suffice to illustrate this phenomenon. A study conducted in the state of Washington found that the job of a licensed practical nurse required skill, effort, and responsibility equivalent to that of a campus police officer. In 1978 the state paid the former an average monthly salary of $739 and the latter $1,070. Similarly, researchers at the University of Wisconsin found that the U.S. Department of Labor rated dog pound attendants and zoo workers more highly than nursery school teachers or day care workers. The researchers suggested that important characteristics of child care work were not regarded as job-related skills but rather as qualities intrinsic to being a woman.[49] The evidence shows a magic circle in which women are paid less because they perform women's jobs, and women's jobs are paid less because they are performed by women.

Women's participation in the job market is characterized by their disproportionate concentration in a small number of relatively routine, low-skilled, and poorly paid occupations and in lower job levels within individual occupations. This is only partially explained by overt or covert discrimination. Equal participation is also inhibited by a structural incompatibility of the labor market with child care and household responsibilities, still largely borne by women rather than men. Approximately one-third of working mothers are employed on a part-time basis, which is significantly underpaid in comparison with full-time employment and lacks proportionate fringe benefits and promotion opportunities.[50] The structural incompatibility reflects the ideological separation of the economic and domestic spheres.

Inherent in the scheme is a failure to acknowledge the economic value of traditional female labor. The fact that domestic labor goes unpaid when performed for a woman's own household appears critical in the general undervaluation of women's labor. The exchange value of female labor power in the market is determined largely by the fact that they draw no income from their labor within the home. Unequal pay is a direct result of the unpaid domestic and reproductive services of all women, whether they engage exclusively in child care and housework or also perform professional work.[51]

The Value of Reproductive Labor

Although the economic value of reproductive activity is obscured by the altruistic ethic governing domestic relations, national population policies—operating in the public sphere—acknowledge its political-economic or demographic aspects. Officially, human life may not be a commodity, but it is the core economic resource of any society.[52] The exclusion of domestic reproductive labor from the public economy is the ultimate manifestation of a patriarchal double standard. "Fatherhood," says O'Brien, "is a paradigm case of getting something for nothing."[53] The entire economic order rests on the foundation that women perform the services necessary to produce the next generation in exchange for support by their husbands, or for nothing.[54]

It seems clear that the imposition of "wages for reproduction" as a universal norm would profoundly upset the present system of a monetary economy. Indeed, the peculiar self-generative quality of money might be intrinsically related to the norm of unpaid female reproductive activity. Capitalist property seems to operate much as biological paternity on a self-generating principle of male continuity. The artificial principle of patrilineal kinship translates biological relations into property relations. Capital has the capacity to reproduce and multiply itself without recourse to sexuality and without any need for females.[55]

Is it, then, the case that money reproduces itself because female reproductive activity is not evaluated in monetary terms? Are we all getting richer from the surplus value of the free labor of childbearing women? If so, is not the prohibition of payment for "surrogate" reproductive services tantamount to moralized slavery?

Slavery is, indeed, suggested by the often-made analogy between surrogate motherhood and biblical concubinage, as in the cases of Abram and Sarai and Hagar, and of Jacob and Rachel and Bilhah, and Leah and Zilpah.[56] In fact, the analogy is not well taken. Although the concubine performed a function similar to that of the surrogate mother, producing an heir for a man in place of a childless wife, she remained responsible for the rearing of the child. More important, the legal status of concubines is radically different. Whereas the surrogate is a free person, the concubine of the Bible was the slave of the patriarch's wife and the property of the patriarch as a member of his extended household.[57]

The free personality of the surrogate mother is nowhere more apparent than where she puts an economic price on her reproductive activity. The perception that she is selling a child (a possession) stems from an objectification of the end product of her activity rather than from the activity's intrinsic value. Human reproductive activity is distinct from that of animals in its consciousness, its imagination, and its purpose. The value of human reproductive labor is distinct from that inhering potentially in the child and is specific to the female reproductive capacity. It is the "synthetic" value of what O'Brien calls "the unity of sentient beings with natural process and the integrity of the continuity of the race," as opposed to the alienation of men from their seed.[58] This value, mediated by the human personality of the reproducing woman, is the source of the qualitative difference between the surrogate mother and the incubator.

The biological function of motherhood has been conceptualized as an insurmountable biohistorical fact. It has served as the root of a causal chain that goes: "maternity, family, absence from production and public life, sexual inequality."[59] According to this scheme, woman is grounded inescapably in her biological nature. As Simone de Beauvoir put it: "Woman has ovaries, a uterus; these peculiarities imprison her in her subjectivity, circumscribe her within the limits of her own nature."[60]

I was alerted to the complex issue of surrogate mother arrangements because of the overwhelming opposition that I found in the literature to their legality and morality. In exploring the matter I discovered that the activity poses a radical challenge to fundamental notions in patriarchal ideology, amid a rapidly developing technology that appears to perpetuate those very notions. The surrogate mother conceives intentionally; she bears a child outside the bounds of marriage; she refutes openly the nexus of biological and social motherhood; and she claims a right to participate in the market economy in this regard. She implies that we women, as human beings, are capable of exercising reason with respect to reproduction and of sharing our birth power with those less fortunate than we.

This is obviously a symbolic portrait. Real-life surrogate mothers are not involved in any radical political movement. Their reproductive consciousness is colored by existing cultural values as much as that of those who would wish them to disappear overnight or, at least, to labor free of charge as altruistic volunteers.

I have attempted here to bring to light some motifs that explain the strong condemnation of commercial surrogacy arrangements and to point to a possible break from the bonds of a gender-differentiated ideology through a transformation in reproductive consciousness.

In spite of the focus on the commercial aspect of surrogacy, the real issue is the power to control human reproduction. The idea of an enforceable contract is based on the notion of autonomous responsible persons making promises binding on themselves before the life of the child at stake ever begins its process of coming into being. The commercial context is merely contingent; commodification of the child-to-be and disrespect for its potential personality are in no way intrinsic to contract. Ours is a culture, however, that attaches power to control of the purse strings. If women are to claim power over reproduction in an age of science and technology, it is only rational that they come to terms with the seemingly repulsive notion of putting an economic price on reproductive activity.

Responsibility or accountability are key to positions of power. If we are to transform our patriarchal reproductive consciousness, we cannot evade the burden of our personal human agency. Far from advocating a revolution, all I am suggesting is that responsibility for reproductive decisions—both "right" and "wrong" ones—be left to the discretion of the individual, regardless of gender. Knowledge is the sum of our experience. We need not fear our experiments so long as we hold ourselves personally accountable for their consequences.

NOTES

Chapter 1: Introduction

1. The facts of the *Baby M* case as presented here are adapted from the findings of Judge Sorkow at the trial. See *In re Baby M,* 217 N.J. Super. 313, 13 *Fam. L. Rep.* (BNA) 2001 (1987).

2. The term *common law* refers here to the system of law that the colonies in North America brought with them from England. The system developed in England as the king extended control over his realm through judges who went on periodic circuit trips to resolve disputes on a case-by-case basis according to local custom. Eventually there came into being a body of law that was "common" to the entire land and was extended to individual cases as a matter of precedent. "Common law" is also used in a narrower sense to distinguish rules of law that have their origin in judicial decisions from those that are enacted in statutes by legislatures.

3. The Committee to Consider the Social, Ethical and Legal Issues Arising from In Vitro Fertilization (chaired by Professor Louis Waller, Law Reform Commissioner), 1984 Report on the Disposition of Embryos Produced by In Vitro Fertilization, secs. 4.6, .11–.17.

4. 1984 Report of the Committee of Inquiry into Human Fertilisation and Embryology (chaired by Dame Mary Warnock) (London, HMSO, Cmnd. 9314), sec. 8.18.

5. Id., secs. 8.10–12.

6. Id., secs. 8.10–12, .17.

7. *In the Matter of Baby M,* 14 *Fam. L. Rep.* (BNA) 2008 (1988).

8. Id., at 2017.

9. Id., at 2018.

10. P. Chesler, *Sacred Bond: The Legacy of Baby M* 109 (1988).

11. See, e.g., Oakley, Fertility Control—A Woman's Issue, 4 *J. Ob. Gyn.* S1 (1984). Cf. D. F. Feldman, *Birth Control in Jewish Law* 169–248 (1968), for Talmudic discussions of contraception.

12. Three points can be made in this respect: (1) Neither genetic engineering nor extrauterine conception and gestation are sufficient causes of a

totalitarian political structure. (2) Manipulation of human beings is not in the exclusive realm of biomedical technology. Plato's *Republic* suggests as forceful a social engineering program aimed at an ideal state in which each individual knows his place. (3) There is no necessary logical connection between extrauterine conception or gestation and genetic manipulation. Questions of positive and negative eugenic policies are indeed of great concern, but can be discussed on a separate level from issues of noncoital reproduction.

13. A. C. Scales, The Emergence of Feminist Jurisprudence: An Essay, 95 *Yale L.J.* 1373 (1986).

14. S. de Beauvoir, *The Second Sex* 58–59 (1949; reprint 1968).

15. M. O'Brien, *The Politics of Reproduction* 21–22, 29–30 (1981). O'Brien attributes the discovery of contraception to modern technology, but as already mentioned nonscientific methods of contraception were available in ancient cultures. In any event, the precise timing of these historical moments is immaterial to the point that both exemplify a conceptualization of causality in reproduction.

16. Id., at 53.

17. Robertson, Procreative Liberty and the Control of Conception, Pregnancy, and Childbirth, 69 *Va. L. Rev.* 405, 406 (1983).

18. H. S. Maine, *Ancient Law* 139–40 (1861; reprint 1986). Interestingly enough, this dictum comes at the conclusion of a comprehensive analysis of the patriarchal family in ancient law.

19. M. A. Glendon, *The New Family and the New Property* 42 (1981).

20. Maine, at 105–09.

21. H. D. Kirk, *Adoptive Kinship: A Modern Institution in Need of Reform* xvi (1981).

22. E. Fromm, *The Art of Loving* 107–09 (1957).

Chapter 2: The Biological Family

1. 49 D.L.R. 15 (1921), at 20.

2. Compare Petz, Artificial Insemination: Legal Aspects, 34 *U. Det. L.J.* 404, 424 (1957).

3. Instruction on Respect for Human Life in Its Origin and on the Dignity of Procreation, Rome, Feb. 22, 1987. The full text of this doctrinal statement was published in the *New York Times*, Mar. 11, 1987, at A14.

4. F. Engels, *The Origin of the Family, Private Property and the State* chap. 2 (1884; reprint 1942).

5. S. de Beauvoir, *The Second Sex* chap. 5 (1949; reprint 1968).

6. For variations on this theme see further M. O'Brien, *The Politics of Reproduction* 52–56 (1981), and G. Greer, *Sex and Destiny: The Politics of Human Fertility* 37–39 (1984).

7. Under common law the married woman was incapable of owning, acquiring, or disposing of property. See W. Blackstone, *Commentaries on the Laws of England,* bk. 1, chaps. 15, 29.

8. See Engels, at 129–30. Beauvoir, at 94, cites Arthur Schopenhauer: "Prostitutes are human sacrifices on the altar of monogamy"; cf. id., 523–24.

9. "In American patriarchy, all women are believed to embody sexual evil. Sexual racism has caused black women to bear the brunt of society's need to degrade and devalue women. While white women have been placed on a pedestal, black women are seen as fallen women. . . . Negative attitudes towards black women were the result of prevailing racist-sexist stereotypes that portrayed black women as morally impure. Many white women felt that their status as ladies would be undermined were they to associate with black women." B. Hooks, *Ain't I a Woman? Black Women and Feminism* 110, 130 (1981). Cf. J. Weeks, *Sex, Politics, and Society: The Regulation of Sexuality since 1800* 19–30 (1981).

10. H. D. Krause, *Illegitimacy: Law and Social Policy* 83 (1971).

11. Compare Beauvoir, at 159ff. See also A. Dworkin, *Right-Wing Women* (1983), for an elaboration on these themes to explain contemporary antifeminist attitudes among women.

12. H. Cohn, *Human Rights in Jewish Law* 168–69 (1984); Z. Falk, Jewish Family Law, *International Encyclopedia of Comparative Law,* vol. 4 (1983), chap. 11, pp. 35–36, 49.

13. F. Pollock and F. Maitland, *The History of English Law,* 2d ed., 2:374, 393–94, 484, 544 (1959).

14. S. Maidment, *Child Custody and Divorce: The Law in Social Context* 110–21 (1984); J. Eekelaar, *Family Law and Social Policy* 7, 31 (1978).

15. H. H. Clark, *The Law of Domestic Relations* 328, 585, 630 (1968). A double standard of sexual propriety persists in present-day custody suits. Cf., e.g., these two cases: *Jarrett v. Jarrett,* 400 N.E.2d 421 (1980) (change of custody predicated on open and continuing cohabitation of mother with boyfriend), and *Simmons v. Simmons,* Kan., 576 P.2d 589 (1978) (change of custody awarded to father despite extramarital sexual relationship).

16. Clark, at 262–68.

17. Comment, Artificial Insemination: A Parvenu Intrudes on Ancient Law, 58 *Yale L.J.* 457 (1949), 461–65; L. Young, *Out of Wedlock* 3 (1954).

18. Krause, at 2–4, 12–13. Cf. *Loving v. Va.* 388 U.S. 1 (1967) (statute prohibiting miscegenous marriage held unconstitutional); *Weber v. Aetna Casualty and Surety Co.* 406 U.S. 164 (1972) (statutory discrimination against miscegenous bastard held unconstitutional).

19. Hankins, Illegitimacy, Social Aspects, 7 *Ency. Soc. Sci.* 580–81 (1932).

20. Young, at 218–19.

21. Krause, at 270–72; Young, at 10–11; Dworkin, at 165–69. The Aid to Families with Dependent Children (AFDC) program has been much criticized for discriminating against black women. Illegitimacy rates among blacks are higher than among whites: in 1977, 79.4 as opposed to 13.7 per 1,000 unmarried women aged fifteen to forty-four in the United States. I. L. Reiss, *Family Systems in America,* 3d ed., 207–13 (1980). Indeed, both sexism and racism impose social restrictions on persons on grounds of biological inferiority. The concept of blood goes beyond its use in defining family membership to determine the boundaries of race that may not be crossed in marriage or reproduction. See, e.g., B. Hooks, *Feminist Theory: From Margin to Center* 52 (1984): "The very concept of white supremacy relies on the perpetuation of a white race. It is in the interest of continued white racist domination of the planet for white patriarchy to maintain control over all women's bodies."

22. E. Schur, *Labeling Women Deviant: Gender Based Stigma as Social Control* 83–84 (1984); Young, at 5–6.

23. Krause, at 25–42. A series of Supreme Court decisions have held statutory distinctions between legitimate and illegitimate children unconstitutional. See, e.g., *Levy v. La.* 391 U.S. 68 (1969) and *Glona v. Am. Guar. and Liab. Ins. Co.* 391 U.S. 73 (1968) (wrongful death); *Labine v. Vincent* 401 U.S. 532 (1971) and *Trimble v. Gordon* 430 U.S. 762 (1977) (inheritance); *Stanley v. Ill.* 405 U.S. 645 (1972) (guardianship); *Weber v. Aetna Casualty and Sur. Co.* 406 U.S. 164 (1972) (workers' compensation); *Gomez v. Perez* 409 U.S. 535 (1973) (child support).

24. Krause, at 105–09, 121–22; Clark, at 162–67.

25. Compare *Mills v. Habluetzel* 456 U.S. 91 (1982), where the Supreme Court struck down a one-year statute of limitations for paternity actions as being an unconstitutional restriction on the rights of illegitimate children. "The unwillingness of the mother to file a paternity action on behalf of her

child, which could stem . . . from the emotional strain of having an illegitimate child, or even from the desire to avoid community and family disapproval, may continue years after the child is born." Per O'Connor, J., at
105.

26. Tests for genetic factors in red blood cells establish a cumulative
probability of exclusion of 62 percent for randomly selected white men and
57 percent for blacks. Testing for markers in white blood cells, which at
present comprise more than fifty known factors (HLA), establishes a probability of exclusion of 90 percent for whites and 88 percent for blacks. The
cumulative probability of exclusion rises to 96 percent when both red and
white cell tests are used. Ellman and Kaye, Probabilities and Proof: Can
HLA and Blood Group Testing Prove Paternity? 54 *N.Y.U. L. Rev.* 1131,
1138–41 (1979); Reisner and Bolk, A Layman's Guide to the Use of Blood
Group Analysis in Paternity Testing, 20 *J. Fam. L.* 657, 666, 671 (1982).

27. Krause, at 127–36; Reisner and Bolk, at 672; Ellman and Kaye, at
1146–61; Joint AMA-ABA Guidelines: Present Status of Serologic Testing
in Problems of Disputed Parentage, 10 *Fam. L. Q.* 247, 260–63 (1976);
Jaffee, Comment on the Judicial Use of HLA Paternity Test Results and
Other Statistical Evidence, 17 *J. Fam. L.* 457 (1979). According to the Joint
AMA-ABA Guidelines, at 260, the great majority of paternity disputes are
"one-man" cases, that is, only one man is named the putative father and he
is not excluded by blood tests.

28. Ellman and Kaye, at 1159.

29. For example, Norway, West Germany, East Germany, Poland, and
Czechoslovakia. See Krause, Creation of Relationships of Kinship, 4 *International Encyclopedia of Comparative Law,* chap. 6, secs. 80, 81.

30. 405 U.S. 645 (1972).

31. 441 U.S. 380 (1979).

32. In that case nothing in the record indicated that either parent was more
responsible for the care of their two daughters, except for a period of nine
months when they lived with the mother and regularly visited the father.
Both parents had filed for adoption by their new spouses. The court divided
five to four in recognizing the father's right to veto an adoption, despite its
uniform acknowledgment of the *general* rule that the mother-child relation
was more intimate than the father-child relation. Consistent with this approach, in *Lehr v. Robertson* 103 Sup. Ct. 2985 (1983), a father who failed
to develop a relationship with his daughter was not allowed to veto her
adoption by the mother's new husband. Cf. *Quilloin v. Walcott* (434 U.S.
268 [1978]) rejecting a challenge to an adoption statute requiring consent of

married fathers and not of unmarried fathers, since no real father-child relationship had been established in the case before the court.

33. 441 U.S. 347 (1979).

34. Per Stevens, J. (dissenting), in *Caban v. Mohammed,* at 408.

35. Per Stevens, J., in *Lehr v. Robertson,* at 2993.

36. Compare Law, Rethinking Sex and the Constitution, 132 *U. Pa. L. Rev.* 955, 990–96 (1984).

Chapter 3: Adoption

1. H. S. Maine, *Ancient Law* 101–10 (1861; reprint 1986).

2. M. K. Benet, *The Politics of Adoption* 29–31 (1976).

3. Id., at 70–72.

4. Id., at 65–68. Garrison, Why Terminate Parental Rights? 35 *Stan. L. Rev.* 423, 434–40 (1983). Some children were neither indentured nor institutionalized but placed in homes. But there was little consideration of the care they would receive there. Between 1853 and 1880 one "child rescue" agency, the New York Children's Aid Society, sent thousands of children by train from New York City to the West, where they were handed over to anyone who wanted a child.

5. Benet, at 14, 76. Rosalind Petchesky argues that the doctrine of the state as *parens patriae* and the principle of parental autonomy have always been applied selectively along lines of class and that prejudice against the poor still pervades our norms of reproduction and parenthood, especially with respect to sterilization and abortion. Petchesky, *Abortion and Woman's Choice: The State, Sexuality, and Reproductive Freedom* 84–96, 155–61, 304–05 (1984).

6. B. Lifton, *Lost and Found* 212–13 (1979); Petchesky, at 209.

7. S. Arms, *To Love and Let Go* 18 (1983); Lifton, at 45.

8. Patti Baker (Natural Mother) in J. Shawyer, *Death by Adoption* 130–31 (1979).

9. L. Young, *Out of Wedlock* 28–39 (1954).

10. Compare Petchesky, at 208–10, for the argument that the opposition to freedom of abortion, specifically with respect to teenage pregnancy, is part of a politics that seeks to curtail the free expression of female sexuality. A large-scale study conducted in the 1950s showed that the familial background and personality characteristics of unwed mothers did not differ significantly from what would be found generally among women of similar

race and age. E. Schur, *Labeling Women Deviant: Gender Based Stigma as Social Control* 84 (1984). Likewise, a British study following all the children born in one week of 1958 found no difference in social class between the parents of legitimate and illegitimate children or between the mothers who kept their babies and those who gave them up. Benet, at 173.

11. Lifton, at 210–21.

12. Shawyer, at 16.

13. Sue (Natural Mother), in id., at 152.

14. A relatively recent study of the treatment single pregnant women receive from doctors, nurses, and social workers found that although these professionals articulate a belief in "maternal instinct," they do not hold this to apply to unmarried women. They view single motherhood as neither medically nor socially desirable. See M. Barrett, Female Sexuality, in *Human Sexual Relations: Towards a Redefinition of Sexual Politics* 310, at 319 (Brake, ed., 1982).

15. Lifton, at 216.

16. Shawyer, at 23, 152–53. According to one comprehensive study of adoption, over half of the birth mothers reported some upsetting element in the surrender process, including the cold, impersonal atmosphere of the procedure, pressure into signing against her real wishes, trouble that the decision was irrevocable and she would never know about or see the child again, and general discomfort in an emotional situation. W. Meezan, S. Katz, and E. Russo, *Adoptions without Agencies: A Study of Independent Adoptions* 105 (1977).

17. Lifton, at 210.

18. Id., at 208; Benet, at 172–75.

19. Benet, at 92–93.

20. See, e.g., Tartanella, Sealed Adoption Records and the Constitutional Right of Privacy of the Natural Parent, 34 *Rutgers L. Rev.* 451 (1982); Kilbanoff, Genealogical Information in Adoption: The Adoptee's Quest and the Law, 11 *Fam. L. Q.* 185 (1977). The court records contain limited information about the child's medical and residential history from birth to adoption. They are unlikely to include any information that identifies the birth family or the reasons for relinquishment. Yet adoption agency records might include a description and medical history of the birth mother, information about the circumstances of surrender, and a report on the adoptive parents' suitability. Although agency files are not necessarily covered by the sealed records statutes, the general policy is not to disclose their content.

21. Unruh, Adoptee's Equal Protection Rights, 28 *UCLA L. Rev.* 1314 1322–27 (1981).

22. Sparks, Adoption: Sealed Adoption Record Laws—Constitutional Violation or a Need for Judicial Reform? 35 *Okla. L. Rev.* 575, 578 (1982). Cf. Kilbanoff, at 188; Tartanella, at 181–82; Unruh, at 1340–42.

23. Sparks, at 579, also notes a racial component in the closed model of adoption and in the changed mores, since many children placed for adoption were the offspring of interracial relationships.

24. Lifton, at 14.

25. Lifton, On the Adoption Experience, *Foreword* to Benet, at 1–2. Daniel Defoe vividly presented the incest taboo and the abhorrence it engenders in *Moll Flanders,* in which the heroine unwittingly marries her own brother: "I lived therefore in open avowed incest and whoredom, and all under the appearance of an honest wife; and though I was not much touched with the crime of it, yet the action had something in it shocking to nature, and made my husband, as he thought himself, even nauseous to me."

26. A. D. Sorosky et al., *The Adoption Triangle: The Effects of the Sealed Record on Adoptees, Birth Parents, and Adoptive Parents* 88–89 (1978).

27. H. D. Kirk, *Adoptive Kinship: A Modern Institution in Need of Reform* 8–9, 23, 30–34 (1981).

28. Garrison, at 465–66; Benet, at 189–91.

29. Benet, at 181–89.

30. Sparks, at 581–82; Kilbanoff, at 193; Sorosky et al., at 110–14; Petchesky, at 223–27.

31. Sorosky et al., at 110–14; Petchesky, at 223–27.

31. Sorosky et al., at 121–42; Lifton (1979), at 78.

32. Sparks, at 581; Unruh, at 1348–49; Sorosky et al., at 73.

33. Sorosky et al., at 222–23.

34. Id., at 50–54.

35. Shawyer, at 22.

36. According to a survey cited in *ALMA Soc'y v. Mellon* 601 F.2d, 1225, 1233 (note 13) (1979), 128 out of 152 birth parents selected at random were willing to meet with adoptees. The Juvenile Rights Project of the American Civil Liberties Union Foundation reported a 1979 study of reunions which showed that 90 percent of the adoptees were satisfied with the outcome of the reunion and that 82 percent of the birth parents had been "positive and accepting." Another study of reunions found that 87 percent of the parties declared they were glad that they had met, and only 2 percent considered the reunion unsuccessful. See 5 *Fam. L. Rep.* (BNA) 2502–03 (1979).

37. Sorosky et al., at 49.

38. *Mills v. Atlantic City Dep't of Vital Statistics*, 148 N.J. Super. 302, 307 A.2d 646 (1977); *ALMA Soc'y Inc. v. Mellon*, 459 F. Supp. 912 (SDNY 1978); aff'd 601 F.2d 1225 (2d cir.); cert. denied 444 U.S. 995 (1979); *Application of Maples*, 563 S.W.2d 760 (Mo. 1978); *Application of Gilbert*, 563 S.W.2d 768 (Mo. 1978); *Application of Sage*, 21 Wash. App. 803, 586 P.2d 1201 (1978); *In re Roger B.*, 84 Ill.2d 323, 418 N.E.2d 751 (1981); *Linda F. M. v. Dep't of Health of the City of New York*, 52 N.Y.2d 236, 418 N.E.2d 1302 (1981).

39. "Conflicts over secrecy . . . are conflicts over power: the power that comes through controlling the flow of information. . . . True, power requires not only knowledge but the capacity to put knowledge to use; but without the knowledge, there is no chance to exercise power." S. Bok, *Secrets: On the Ethics of Concealment and Revelation* 19 (1983).

40. Baran, Pannor, and Sorosky, Open Adoption, 31 *Soc. Work* 97 (1976).

41. Garrison, at 423–24; Amadio and Deutsch, Open Adoption: Allowing Children to "Stay in Touch" with Blood Relatives, 22 *J. Fam. L.* 59 (1983), at 79–82.

42. Garrison, at 461–64. Cf. Derdeyn, Rogoff, and Williams, Alternatives to Absolute Termination of Parental Rights after Long-Term Foster Care, 31 *Vand. L. Rev.* 1165 (1978), for details of successful permanent placement with foster parents while permitting visitation by birth parents.

43. See, e.g., *In re Marino*, 30 Cal. App. 952, 106 Cal. Rptr. 655 (1973); *Ross v. Hoffman*, 33 Md. App. 333, 364 A.2d 596 (1976); modified, 280 Md. 172, 372 A.2d 582 (1977); *Bennett v. Marrow*, 59 A.D.2d 492, 399 N.Y.S.2d 637 (1977); *Reflow v. Reflow*, 24 Or. App. 375, 545 P.2d 894 (1976).

44. Section 104(c), 45 Fed. Reg. 10622 (1980).

45. Meezan, Katz, and Russo, at 3, 27–28. Cf. Myers, Independent Adoptions: Is the Black and White Beginning to Appear in the Controversy over Gray-Market Adoptions? 18 *Duquesne L. Rev.* 629 (1980), at 635.

46. According to one study, 34 of the 115 birth mothers interviewed knew the names of the adoptive parents. Of these, 24 knew how to get in touch with them and 9 had direct contact. Forty-four of the mothers reported that the adoptive parents' names were on the consent forms that they signed. Over half of the 131 adoptive parents interviewed knew the name of the birth mother, including 10 couples who had a child placed directly by the mother (Meezan, Katz, and Russo, at 61, 102). The reasons cited by birth mothers for choosing independent placement included: financial-medical needs could not be met in an acceptable way by an agency ($N = 11$), they

did not like or trust the agency worker ($N = 8$), they did not know who the adoptive couple would be and would never see the child ($N = 8$), and they did not want the child to go into foster care ($N = 4$) (id., 108–10). Reasons given for not approaching an agency included the following: there was no need because they were already involved with an intermediary (33 percent), they did not know about agencies (26 percent), agencies were impersonal (11 percent), intrusive of privacy (11 percent), did not allow mothers to choose an adoptive couple (9 percent), and might place the child in foster care (6 percent). Twenty-eight of the 33 women who did approach agencies reported negative experiences, including judgmental, insensitive attitudes ($N = 9$), and excessive or useless counseling ($N = 5$) (id., 10–11, 106–08).

47. Id., at 5, 28, 182–85.

48. Turano, at 48–49; Wallisch, at 333.

49. Meezan, Katz, and Russo, at 28–29; Pritchard, A Market for Babies? 34 *U. Toronto L.J.* 341, 343 (1981).

50. Turano, at 59; Wallisch, at 351; Myers, at 638. Cf. H. H. Clark, *Law of Domestic Relations in the United States* 652, n. 88 (1968).

51. Compare Wisotsky, Exposing the War on Cocaine: The Futility and Destructiveness of Prohibition, 1983 *Wis. L. Rev.* 1305.

52. *In re Estate of Shirk* 186 Kan. 311, 350 P.2d 1, 12 (1960); cf. *Reimche v. First Nat'l Bank of Nev.* 512 F.2d 187 (9th Cir. 1975).

53. Meezan, Katz, and Russo, 97–98.

54. Compare Section 302 of the Model Adoption Act, 45 Fed. Reg. 10622, 10633 (1980). In Europe, too, similar provisions are found. In East Germany and Sweden consent has no legal effect before birth. In England and Switzerland consent is disregarded if given when the child is less than six weeks old. In West Germany and Denmark the child must be at least three months old before a valid consent may be executed. See Krause, *Encyclopedia of International Law*, vol. 4, sec. 6.170–75.

55. Meezan, Katz, and Russo, 158–60; Comment, Revocation of Consent to Adoption Not Allowed in the Absence of Fraud or Duress, 15 *J. Fam. L.* 123 (1976–77). Cf. *Franklin v. Biggs* 14 Or. App. 450, 513 P.2d 1216 (1973), where the court allowed withdrawal of consent that was given in return for cash payments on grounds of public policy.

56. Compare M. O'Brien, *The Politics of Reproduction* 19 (1981): "What [science] shows us is that mammalian reproduction is but one class of animal reproduction. Anything specifically human in the process apparently must await the appearance of the product of the process, the child, as a separate but dependent creature."

57. Benet, at 179; cf. Meezan, Katz, and Russo, at 155; Krause, at 6.169.

58. 45 Fed. Reg. 10622, 10633 (1980). If the father does not relinquish before birth, he must also observe the seventy-two-hour waiting period. Cf. Ill. Rev. Stat., chap. 4, sec. 9.1–9 (1973), for express exclusion of the father from the norm prohibiting prenatal consent.

Chapter 4: Artificial Insemination

1. Kardimon, Artificial Insemination in the Talmud, 2 *Harofe Halvri* 164 (1950); Rohleder, *Test Tube Babies* 30–39 (1934); A. M. Schellen, *Artificial Insemination in the Human* 9 (1957); W. J. Finegold, *Artificial Insemination,* 2d ed., 5–6 (1976).

2. Rohleder, at 130–31. This summary does not include the claim of one French doctor to have treated 567 women with only 67 failures, reported by Schellen, at 17. The same doctor was apparently later condemned for his "doubtful practices."

3. Schellen, at 19–20; Finegold, at 7.

4. Seymour and Koernor, Artificial Insemination: Present Status in the United States as Shown by a Recent Survey, 116 *JAMA* 2747 (1941). See, however, Folsome, The Status of Artificial Insemination: A Critical Review, 45 *Am. J. Ob. Gyn.* 915 (1943), questioning the credibility of these findings because the reported number of successful pregnancies was approximately twenty-one times greater than that reported in the entire medical literature during the previous four decades.

5. Schellen, at 2; Guttmacher, Role of Artificial Insemination in Treatment of Sterility, 15 *Ob. Gyn. Surv.* 767 (1960); Curie-Cohen, Luttrell, and Shapiro, Current Practice of Artificial Insemination by Donor in the United States, 300 *New Eng. J. Med.* 585, 588 (1979).

6. Rohleder.

7. R. W. Wertz and L. C. Wertz, *Lying In* 77–106 (1977); L. Gordon, *Woman's Body, Woman's Right* 24, 64 (1976); J. Reed, *From Private Vice to Public Virtue* 37–39 (1978).

8. Rohleder, at 166–67, 170–72.

9. Id., at 150.

10. Compare Mangin, Symposium on Artificial Insemination: The Social and Anthropological Viewpoint, 7 *Syracuse L. Rev.* 107 (1955).

11. Rohleder, at 96–101.

12. See M. Barrett, Female Sexuality, in *Human Sexual Relations: Towards a Redefinition of Sexual Politics* 320 (Brake, ed., 1982).

13. Schellen, at 276.

14. Ibid., at 150–54; Weisman, The Selection of Donors for Use in Artificial Insemination, 50 *W. J. Surg.* 142 (1942).

15. Weisman, Studies on Human Artificial Insemination, 55 *W. J. Surg.* 348, 351 (1947); Schellen, at 277–78; Strickler, Keller, and Warren, Artificial Insemination with Fresh Donor Sperm, 293 *New Eng. J. Med.* 848 (1975).

16. Rohleder, at 173; Finegold, at 31–32; Seymour and Koernor, at 2748.

17. Curie-Cohen et al., at 586.

18. Note, Artificial Insemination Versus Adoption, 34 *Va. L. Rev.* 822, 825 (1948); Comment, Artificial Insemination: Confusion Compounded, 3 *Wayne L. Rev.* 35 n. 35 (1956); Tallin, Artificial Insemination, 34 *Can. B. Rev.* 1, 6 (1956).

19. Comment, Artificial Insemination: A Parvenu Intrudes on Ancient Law, 58 *Yale L.J.* 457, 465 (1949); Note, Legal and Social Implications of Artificial Insemination, 34 *Iowa L. Rev.* 658, 666, n. 35 (1949).

20. Petz, Artificial Insemination: Legal Aspects, 34 *U. Det. L.J.* 404, 415 (1957); Note, Social and Legal Aspects of Artificial Insemination, 1965 *Wis. L. Rev.* 859, 870; Berger, Couple's Reaction to Male Infertility and Donor Insemination, 137 *Am. J. Psych.* 1047 (1980).

21. According to a 1947 survey of the American Society for the Study of Fertility, 25 of 44 practitioners never mixed sperm. Of the respondents, 84 percent thought it proper for the administering physician to deliver the child himself and to assent to the use of the husband's name as father on the birth certificate. See Guttmacher, Haman, and MacLeod, The Use of Donors for Artificial Insemination, 1 *Fert. Ster.* 264 (1950). Of the practitioners responding to the 1979 Curie-Cohen survey (at 589), 325 used multiple donors in a single cycle. Cf. Ciba Symposium no. 17, *Law and Ethics of Embryo Transfer* 27–40 (1973).

22. But see Horne, Artificial Insemination Donor: An Issue of Ethical and Moral Values, 293 *New Eng. J. Med.* 873, 874 (1975), and P. Creighton, *Artificial Insemination by Donor* 38–41 (1977), for recent criticism of the secrecy policy in terms of the child's welfare.

23. Schellen, at 288.

24. Finegold, at 48–49.

25. Schellen, at 130–32, 212.

26. Lamson, Pinard, and Meaker, Sociologic and Psychological Aspects

of Artificial Insemination with Donor Semen, 145 *JAMA* 1062 (1961); Port-
noy, Artificial Insemination, 7 *Fert. Ster.* 327, 329 (1956); Schellen, at 271,
274; Finegold, at 94.

27. Schellen, at 283.

28. Finegold, at 101.

29. Curie-Cohen et al., 586.

30. Behrman, Artificial Insemination, 10 *Fert. Ster.* 248, 250 (1959);
Finegold, at 31.

31. Weisman (1943), at 143.

32. Curie-Cohen et al., at 586–87.

33. Weisman (1943), at 143–44; Schellen, at 155–62, 309; Finegold, at
38, 124; Guttmacher et al., at 267.

34. Annas, Fathers Anonymous: Beyond the Best Interests of the Sperm
Donor, 14 *Fam. L. Q.* 1, 7 (1980); Schock, The Legal Status of the Semi-
Adopted, 46 *Dickinson L. Rev.* 271, 275 (1942).

35. New York Sanitary Code, sec. 112; Schellen, at 120; Finegold, at
168.

36. Curie-Cohen et al., at 586–87; Schellen, at 120–22.

37. Guttmacher et al., at 769.

38. Finegold, at 30, 42–43.

39. Curie-Cohen et al., at 589.

40. Lovset, Artificial Insemination: The Attitude of Patients in Norway,
2 *Fert. Ster.* 415, 420–21 (1951).

41. Farris and Garrison, Emotional Impact of Successful Donor Insemination, 3 *Ob. Gyn.* 19 (1954).

42. Section 4.12 of the Report of the Committee of Inquiry into Human
Fertilisation and Embryology (London, HMSO, Cmnd. 9314, 1984). Cf.
the Report on Donor Gametes in IVF, by the Australian Waller Committee
to Consider the Social and Legal Issues Arising from In Vitro Fertilisation
(August 1983), secs. 3.29–36. Both Committees recommended that on
reaching maturity the child should have access to information about his or
her genetic origins.

43. Waller Report, app. A, Dissenting Statement by Dr. Harman.

44. R. Titmuss, *The Gift Relationship* (1971).

45. Warnock Report, sec. 4.27; Waller Report, sec. 3.10.

46. Haman, Results in Artificial Insemination, 72 *J. Urol.* 557 (1954).

47. Curie-Cohen et al., at 586–87.

48. R. Snowden and G. D. Mitchell, *The Artificial Family: A Consideration of Artificial Insemination by Donor* 70 (1983).

49. Finegold, at 34.

50. Wayne Comment, at 43.

51. Schellen, at 282, 310; Tallin, at 6; Yale Comment, at 462; Kelly, Artificial Insemination: Theological and Natural Law Aspects, 33 *U. Det. L.J.* 135 (1956), at 143.

52. Kelly, at 144.

53. Dunstan, Moral and Social Issues Arising from AID, in Ciba Symposium, 52.

54. Ciba Symposium, 58–59.

55. A recent survey of 39 sperm donors indicates some change in attitude. Money was, indeed, the most mentioned reason for donating sperm. Eighty-two percent thought an adopted child should have the right to discover his or her biological parents, and 48 percent believed that the artificial insemination child should have a similar right of discovery. Twenty-one percent felt some responsibility toward a child produced by their sperm, although the nature and extent of the perceived responsibility differed. Marik and Fidell, Characteristics and Attitudes of Sperm Donors, 41 *Fert. Ster.* 107S (1984).

56. Bogdan, Artificial Insemination in Swedish Law, 10 *Comp. L. Yearbook* 91, 96–97 (Center for International Legal Studies, 1986).

57. See, e.g., H. H. Clark, *The Law of Domestic Relations* 156, 172–73 (1968).

58. *Hoch v. Hoch* No. 44-C-9307, Cir. Ct., Cook Co., Ill., 1945.

59. Dienes, Artificial Donor Insemination: Perspectives on Legal and Social Change, 54 *Iowa L. Rev.* 253, 258 (1968). Similar circumstances obtained in the first Canadian case of *Orford v. Orford,* 58 *Dom. L. Rev.* 251 (1921) and in the first Scottish case of *McLennan v. McLennan* (1958) S.C. 105.

60. *Doornbos v. Doornbos* No. 54 S-1498, Super. Ct., Cook Co., Ill., 1954.

61. See Tallin, at 15–16.

62. *People v. Sorenson* 68 Cal.2d 280, 437 P.2d 495 (1968).

63. *Obiter dictum* is a technical term signifying that the court's ruling was not strictly necessary to the resolution of the dispute at bar and therefore does not constitute a binding precedent. In this case the court had established the husband's duty of child support on independent grounds. See text to n. 61, below.

64. 437 P.2d at 501.

65. Holdings for legitimacy: *Strnad v. Strnad* 78 N.Y.S.2d 390, 392

(1948); *People v. Sorenson* 437 P.2d at 501; *In re Adoption of Anonymous* 345 N.Y.S.2d 430, 435 (1973). Holdings for illegitimacy: *Doornbos v. Doornbos; People v. Dennett* 184 N.Y.S.2d 178, 183 (1958) (obiter dictum); *Gursky v. Gursky* 242 N.Y.S.2d 406, 411 (1963); *Anonymous v. Anonymous* 246 N.Y.S.2d 835, 836 (1964).

66. 78 N.Y.S.2d at 391–92.

67. 184 N.Y.S.2d at 182–83.

68. 242 N.Y.S.2d at 411–12.

69. 437 P.2d at 498.

70. Id., at 499.

71. 345 N.Y.S.2d at 434. It is unclear on what basis the court stated that the doctor in this specialty is "often" a woman, but the point is also valid if the doctor is "sometimes" a woman.

72. S. 801 172d Sess. (1949); S. 745 174th Sess. (1951); see *In re Adoption of Anonymous* 345 N.Y.S.2d at 432.

73. Dienes, at 298–303.

74. Alaska Stat. 25.20.045; Ark. Stat. Ann. 61–141; Cal. Civ. Code 7005; Colo. Rev. Stat. 19–6–106; Conn. Gen. Stat. 45–69f; Fla. Stat. Ann. 742.11; Ga. Code Ann. 74–101.1, 74.9904; Ill. Ann. Stat. 40–1451; Kan. Stat. Ann. 23–128; La. Civ. Code Ann. 188; Md. Est. & Trusts Code Ann. 1–206(b); Mich. Comp. Laws Ann. 333.2824, 700.111; Minn. Stat. Ann. 257.56; Mont. Rev. Code Ann. 40–6–106; Nev. Rev. Stat. 126.061; N.Y. Dom. Rel. Law 73; N.C. Gen. Stat. 49A–1; Okla. Stat. Ann. 10–109.239, 677.335; Tenn. Cod. Ann. 53–446; Tex. Fam. Code Ann. 12.03; Va. Code 64.1–7.1; Wash. Rev. Code Ann. 26.26.050; Wis. Stat. Ann. 767.47(9), 891.40; Wyo. Stat. 14–2–103.

75. *C. M. v. C. C.* 377 A.2d 821 (1977).

76. *K. S. v. G. S.* N.J. Super., 440 A.2d 64 (1981).

77. *R. S. v. R. S.* 670 P.2d 923 (Kan. App. 1983).

78. L. M. S. v. S. L. S. Wis. App., 312 N.W.2d 853 (1983).

79. *Byers v. Byers* Okla., 618 P.2d 930 (1980).

80. *In re Adoption of McFadyen* Ill. App., 438 N.E. 2d 1362 (1982).

81. *State ex rel H. v. P.* 457 N.Y.S.2d 488 (A.D. 1982).

Chapter 5: Surrogate Mother Arrangements

1. See, e.g., Erickson, Contracts to Bear a Child, 65 *Cal. L. Rev.* 611, 714 (1978); Harris, Artificial Insemination and Surrogate Motherhood: A

Nursery Full of Unresolved Questions, 17 *Willamette L. Rev.* 913, 951 (1981).

2. 362 N.W.2d 211 (Mich. 1985), reversing 333 N.W.2d 90 (Mich. Ct. App. 1983).

3. 333 N.W.2d at 92.

4. (Ky. Cir. Ct. Jefferson Co.) 9 *Fam. L. Rep.* (BNA) 2348 (1983).

5. See, e.g., sec. 5 of the Uniform Parentage Act; Alaska Stat. 20.20.010 (1975); Colo. Rev. Stat. 19–6–106 (1978); Conn. Gen. Stat. 45–69(g) (1981); Minn. Stat. Ann. 257.56 (1980); Mont. Rev. Code Ann. 40–6–106 (1981); Okla. Stat. Ann. 10–24–551 (1980); Or. Rev. Stat. 677.360 (1979); Va. Code 64.1–7.1 (1979); Wis. Stat. Ann. 891.40 (1980); Wyo. Stat. 14–2–103 (1978). But see Or. Rev. Stat. 677.365 (1979): "Artificial insemination shall not be performed upon a woman without her prior written request and consent and, *if she is married,* the prior written request and consent of her husband" (emphasis added).

6. See Robertson, Procreative Liberty and the Control of Conception, Pregnancy, and Childbirth, 69 *Va. L. Rev.* 405, 430, at n. 67 (1983).

7. See Harris, at 932–37; Kritchevsky, The Unmarried Woman's Right to Artificial Insemination: A Call for an Expanded Definition of Family, 4 *Harv. Women's L.J.* 1 (1981). An analogous question arises as to the participation of single persons (male or female) as the sponsoring parent in a surrogacy arrangement. See Martin, Surrogate Motherhood: Contractual Issues and Remedies under Legislative Proposals, 23 *Washburn L.J.* 601, 626–28 (1984); Patterson, Parenthood by Proxy: Legal Implications of Surrogate Birth, 67 *Iowa L. Rev.* 385, 388 (1982).

8. But note that the attorney general at Oklahoma issued an opinion on surrogacy that posited, inter alia, that "as the [artificial insemination] statute makes no provision for permitting an unmarried woman to be artificially inseminated, it follows that the Legislature intended to prohibit such a possibility"; Okla. Atty Gen., Opinion No. 83–162, 9/29/83, 9 *Fam. L. Rep.* (BNA) 2761 (1983).

9. 377 A.2d 821 (1976).

10. This is consistent with the normative tradition that considered the "adulterous bastard" more offensive than the illegitimate child born from a casual relation with an unmarried woman.

11. Compare Waller, Borne for Another, 10 *Monash L. Rev.* 113, 116 (1984): "At the beginning of February 1984, a Sydney woman and her de facto husband were accused of selling their baby for $10,000. They were charged with the specific offence of attempting to make false entries in the

State's birth register. The police stated that the mother entered hospital using the name of the baby buyer. Four days after the delivery the baby was handed over in exchange for a cheque for the agreed amount. The cheque was dishonoured, the baby recovered by the Department of Youth and Community Services, on the ground that it was 'under improper guardianship', and its future made to depend on a judicial order about its custody and care."

    12. See, e.g., Ariz. Rev. Stat. Ann. 8–105(n) (1980); Cal. Civ. Code 224q (1981); Conn. Gen. Stat. Ann. 17–49a (1981); Del. Code Ann. 13–904(2) (1975); Minn. Stat. Ann. 259.22(2)(c) (1981); N.M. Stat. Ann. 40–70–10B (1978); Ohio Rev. Code Ann. 5103.16 (1981); Or. Rev. Stat. 418.300 (1979); R.I. Gen. Laws 15–7–1 (1980); S.D. Cod. Laws 26–6–8 (1976); Wis. Stat. Ann. 48.60(2)(a) (1979).

    13. See Mady, Surrogate Mothers: The Legal Issues, 7 *Am. J. L. Med.* 323, 331 (1981).

    14. 9 *Fam. L. Rep.* (BNA) 2348 (1983).

    15. Mich. App., 307 N.W.2d 438 (1981); lv. den. 414 Mich. 875 (1982); cert. den. 459 U.S. 1183 (1983).

    16. 6 *Fam. L. Rep.* (BNA) 3013 (1980).

    17. *Beal v. Doe* 432 U.S. 438 (1977), *Maher v. Roe* 432 U.S. 464 (1977)—a state is not constitutionally required to fund nontherapeutic abortions under a Medicaid plan; *Poelker v. Doe* 432 U.S. 519 (1977)—a city may provide publicly financed hospital services for childbirth while excluding abortions; *Harris v. McRae* 448 U.S. 297 (1980), *Williams v. Zbaraz* 448 U.S. 358 (1980)—federal reimbursement for abortion expenses incurred by the states under the Medicaid scheme (excepting cases where pregnancy endangers the mother's life or results from rape or incest) is not constitutionally required, nor are states required to fund abortions for which federal reimbursement is unavailable.

    18. Mich. Cir. Ct. Gratiot Co., 14 *Fam. L. Rep.* (BNA) 1161 (1987).

    19. Compare 1982 Okla. Atty Gen. Opinion No. 83–162, 9 *Fam. L. Rep.* (BNA) 2761 (1983); Holder, Surrogate Motherhood: Babies for Fun and Profit, 90(2) *Case and Comment* 3 (1985).

    20. 132 Misc.2d 972, 505 N.Y.S.2d 813 (Sur. 1986).

    21. 704 S.W.2d 209 (Ky. 1986); affg *Ky. v. Surrogate Parenting Associates,* 10 *Fam. L. Rep.* (BNA) 1105 (1983).

    22. The attorney general of Kentucky had previously published an opinion that payment of monetary consideration in a surrogacy situation was illegal. 1981 Ky. Atty Gen. Opinion No. 18, *Fam. L. Rep.* (BNA) 2246 (1981).

23. Compare Parker, Surrogate Motherhood, Psychiatric Screening and Informed Consent, Baby Selling, and Public Policy, 12 *Bull. Am. Acad. Psych. L.* 21, 32–33 (1984).

24. 7 *Fam. L. Rep.* (BNA) 2351 (1981); *N.Y. Times,* June 5, 1981, at A12, col. 1.

25. [1985] *Fam. L. Rep.* 445 (Fam. & C.A. 1978).

26. This case is known as Stiver and Malahoff. Report of the Michigan State Medical Society Task Force on Bioethics, Sept. 6, 1983; Annas and Elias, *In Vitro* Fertilization and Embryo Transfer: Medicolegal Aspects of a New Technique to Create a Family, 17 *Fam. L. Q.* 199, 217–18 (1983); Waller, at 120; Holder, at 4.

27. See Robertson, Surrogate Mothers: Not So Novel After All, 13 *Hastings Center Rep.* 28, 32 (1983); Krimmel, The Case against Surrogate Parenting, 13 *Hastings Center Rep.* 35, 37 (1983).

28. Michigan S. Bill (S-1) (1983). This legislative initiative followed the publicity surrounding the Stiver and Malahoff case.

29. Cal. Ass. Bill 3771 (1982), Sec. 7515; Mich. H. Bill 4114 (S-H-3) (1983), secs. 7(2), (3); Council of District of Columbia Bill 6–152 (1985), sec. 5(c)(5); Kan. S. Bill 485 (1984), sec. 9(b)(2); S.C. H. Bill 3491 (1982), sec. 20–7-3760.

30. *N.Y. Times,* Dec. 13, 1987.

31. Compare P. Atiyah, *An Introduction to the Law of Contract,* 2d ed., 2 (1971).

32. Id., at 92–95.

33. Id., at 198–201.

34. I would suggest that the promise to assume such responsibility does not in itself constitute consideration, since that would amount to relating to the child as a means rather than an end. In other words, I would argue that absent monetary compensation for the surrogate's reproductive services the agreement should not be legally effective or enforceable.

35. For example, wagering contracts, contracts involving the surrender of statutory power, agreements to oust the jurisdiction of the court, contracts in restraint of personal liberty, and contracts in restraint of trade. Atiyah, at 202–14.

36. Id., at 192–94; C. Fried, *Contract as Promise* 92–93 (1981).

37. The study was based on data from 30 surrogate mothers and interviews with over 350 candidates for surrogacy. Parker, The Psychology of the Pregnant Surrogate Mother: A Newly Updated Report of a Longitudinal

Pilot Study (1984) (ms. available from author); id., op. cit., 21. Compare Lerner et al., On the Need to Be Pregnant, 48 *Int'l J. Psych-Anal.* 288 (1967).

37. See sec. 2–601 of the Uniform Commercial Code. Cf. Annas, Making Babies without Sex: The Law and the Profits, 74 *Pub. Health and L.* 1415, 1417 (1984), for the conclusion that commercial surrogacy is morally unacceptable.

38. Atiyah, at 232.

Chapter 6: In Vitro Fertilization

1. Report of the Committee of Inquiry into Human Fertilisation and Embryology (London, HMSO, Cmnd. 9314, 1984) (hereinafter Warnock Report), chap. 11.

2. Id., sec. 11.10.

3. Report of the Ethics Advisory Board (DHEW), chap. 4, 1979 Rptr. H.R.L. II–B–1, 6.

4. Id., at 3.

5. 1979 Rptr. H.R.L. II–B–11, 14.

6. R. Levine, *Ethics and Regulation of Clinical Research* 2–4 (1981); Belmont Report, 44 F.R. 23192 (1979), cited by D. M. Maloney, *Protection of Human Research Subjects: A Practical Guide to Federal Laws and Regulations* 32–33 (1984). Medical activity can also be classified as a "practice for the benefit of others" when a procedure is applied to one person with the expectation that it will enhance the well-being of another. This differs from "practice" only as regards purpose, and it refers otherwise to an accepted routine medical procedure. Blood donation is a classic example (Levine, at 5–6). A woman's participation in an experimental reproductive procedure might be regarded as an act "for the benefit of others," if one considers it as aimed at achieving the benefit of a new human life. But as long as the procedure is in an experimental stage it cannot be classified as a "practice" for the benefit of others.

7. Levine, at 56, 92–93; Parsons, Definitions of Health and Illness in the Light of American Values and Social Structures, in *Patients, Physicians and Illness* 107 (Jaco, ed., 1972).

8. Department of Health and Human Services (previously DHEW) Regulations for Protection of Human Subjects, 45 C.F.R. 46 (1975). See also DHEW Commission, Institutional Review Boards: Report and Recommen-

dations 1–2 (DHEW Publication No. [OS]78–0008, Washington, D.C., 1978).

9. 45 C.F.R. 46.102(g), 111.

10. 45 C.F.R. 46.116(a)(6). Additional requirements of informed consent in "appropriate" cases are a statement that the particular procedure may involve risks currently unforeseeable, the circumstances under which the subject's participation may be terminated by the investigator without the subject's consent, the consequences of a subject's decision to withdraw from research, and the procedure for orderly termination of participation by the subject; 45 C.F.R. 46.116(b).

11. Oakley presents a parody that exemplifies how generally accepted risks of female contraception would be considered totally unacceptable in a male method of contraception. The parody introduces the findings of a study conducted on 763 male undergraduates as regards an intrapenile device which is inserted through the head of the penis and pushed into the scrotum with a plungerlike device. Experiments on white whales proved the method to be 100 percent effective in preventing the production of sperm, without interfering with the female's rutting pleasure. The researchers declared the method to be statistically safe for human males—only 2 of the tested undergraduates died of scrotal infection, only 20 developed swelling of the testicles, and only 13 were too depressed to have an erection. Common complaints of cramping, bleeding, and acute abdominal pains were regarded merely as indications that the man's body had not yet adjusted to the device. One complication—massive scrotal infection necessitating the surgical removal of the testicles—was considered too rare to be statistically important. The parody concludes with the statement that the benefits of the method far outweighed the risk to any individual man. Oakley, Fertility Control—A Woman's Issue? 4 *J. Ob. Gyn.* S1, S3 (1984).

12. 45 C.F.R. 46.201–11. See, in particular, secs. 46.201(b), 208(b), and 209(d): "An activity permitted under . . . this section may be conducted only if the mother and father are legally competent and have given their informed consent."

13. Report of the Ethics Advisory Board (DHEW), 1979 Rptr. H.R.L. II–B–6.

14. G. Corea, *The Mother Machine: Reproductive Technologies from Artificial Insemination to Artificial Wombs* 113–17, 156–57 (1985).

15. P. Singer and D. Wells, *The Reproductive Revolution: New Ways of Making Babies* 13–17, 23–25 (1984); Jones, Family Formation by Fertilisation In Vitro: Now and Then, in *Human Fertility, Health and Food* 3 (1984); Corea, at 120–21, 179–80.

16. A more recently developed technique employs ultrasonography to locate the ripe follicle and retrieve the egg vaginally under local anesthesia. See Singer and Wells, at 14–15; Warnock Report, sec. 5.2.

17. Singer and Wells, at 24–25; Warnock Report, sec. 5.3; Jones, at 10.

18. This in itself can be distressing: "It occurs to me when I have sex that what used to be beautiful and very private is now degraded and terribly public. I bring my charts to the doctor like a child bringing home a report card. Tell me, did I do well? Did I ovulate? Did I have sex at all the right times as you instructed me?" Corea, at 175.

19. Id., 149–51, 173–74. This latter method was also extremely unpleasant: "You're dehydrated. You're only allowed to have a certain amount of liquid a day. Then all of your urine is collected three-hourly. That means day *and* night. You're wakened up at 10:30, at 1:30, at 4:30, at 7:30—all night long and all day long, collecting urine. And you just sit there and wait. That might be two days. That might be four days. I've seen people wait five days. It's a very long wait and you're very thirsty." Id., 175–76.

20. Leeton, Trounson, and Wood, IVF and ET [Embryo Transfer]: What It Is and How It Works, in *Test-Tube Babies* 1, 6 (Walters and Singer, eds., 1982).

21. Corea, at 177.

22. Id., at 167–68.

23. Oakley, at S2, S4.

24. K. Luker, *Abortion and the Politics of Motherhood* 15–18, 30–32 (1984).

25. Oakley, at S4.

26. B. Rothman, *In Labor: Women and Power in the Birthplace* 44–45, 263–64 (1982); E. Shorter, *A History of Women's Bodies* 160–63 (1982).

27. G. Greer, *Sex and Destiny* 11–12 (1984).

28. A. Rich, *Of Woman Born* 172 (1977).

29. A new experimental technique of medical conception achieves the same effect. Embryo transfer (or lavage) is a method by which conception is achieved in a woman's body and the embryo is then flushed and implanted in another woman's uterus for gestation. The first two live births from this technique occurred in January and June 1984 in Victoria, Australia, and Virginia, United States, respectively. Medical indications for the procedure would be ovulatory malfunctioning (in which case an egg donor would be involved) or inability to sustain pregnancy (involving a "womb donor"). Singer and Wells, at 79; Jones, at 3.

30. See, e.g., Annas, Redefining Parenthood and Protecting Embryos, 14 *Hastings Center Rep.* 50 (1984).

31. Waller Committee, *Report on Donor Gametes in IVF* (Victoria, Australia, August 1983), secs. 4.1–2. The Victoria Infertility (Medical Procedures) Act, 1984, which was enacted following the Waller Report, focuses on the professional administration of reproductive procedures and makes no express provision regarding the definition of legal parent-child relations. Sections 12 and 13 of the act, however, address male and female gamete donors in analogous terms and imply that the gestational mother is taken to be the legal mother.

32. Warnock Report, sec. 6.8.

33. Both the Warnock Report (sec. 6.6) and the Waller Committee's *Issues Paper on Donor Gametes in IVF* (Victoria, Australia, April 1983) (sec. 2.11) noted the difference in procedures for obtaining eggs and sperm, but they drew no conclusions from this fact as to normative significance. The new method of vaginal egg retrieval, with the aid of ultrasound technology, is far less intrusive than the surgical laparoscopy.

34. See, e.g., Singer and Wells, at 76.

35. Attempts to use donor eggs in in vitro fertilization began in 1982. That year, fertilized donor ova were implanted in 18 patients. Only one pregnancy resulted and the woman miscarried at ten weeks. Waller Committee, *Issues Paper,* sec. 2.10.

36. Waller Committee, *Report on Donor Gametes in IVF,* sec. 3.24.

37. Corea, at 172–73; Greer, at 65.

Chapter 7: Contracting to Become a Parent

1. Actually, the legal demarcation of family-market is not at all clearcut. For a comprehensive description of its blending, see Olsen, The Family and the Market: A Study of Ideology and Legal Reform, 96 *Harv. L. Rev.* 1497 (1983).

2. S. de Beauvoir, *The Second Sex* 74 (1949; reprint 1968).

3. See *Bradwell v. Ill.* 83 U.S. (16 Wall) 130 (1873), per Bradley, J., for a classic legal restatement of the "pedestal-cage" attitude to the female sex.

4. C. Gilligan, *In a Different Voice* (1982).

5. See, e.g., T. Hobbes, *Leviathan* 185 (1651; reprint 1968): "During the time men live without a common Power to keep them all in awe, they are in that condition which is called Warre; and such a warre, as is of every man, against every man."

6. N. Chodorow, *The Reproduction of Mothering: Psychoanalysis and the Sociology of Gender* 169 (1978).

7. The correlative of a right, in the existing system, is a duty in another person toward the holder of the right. See W. N. Hohfeld, *Fundamental Legal Conceptions* 35–38 (1919). Responsibility derives from a failure to perform one's duty. A person who is found to be responsible for the violation of a right (by an impartial judge) will be held liable to compensate the injured person (civil liability) or society at large (criminal liability).

8. Compare Churchill and Simon, Abortion and the Rhetoric of Individual Rights, 12 *Hastings Center Rep.* 9 (1982).

9. The notion of autonomy rests on the perception that all actions implicate the interests of other persons, whereas that of liberty gives rise to a problematic distinction between self-regarding and other-regarding activities. See J. S. Mill, *On Liberty* 126, 205–25 (1859; reprint 1962). "The only part of the conduct of any one, for which he is amenable to society, is that which concerns others. In the part which merely concerns himself, his independence is, of right, absolute." Id., at 135.

10. *Meyer v. Neb.* 262 U.S. 390 (1923); *Pierce v. Soc'y of Sisters* 268 U.S. 510 (1925); cf. *Moore v. Cleveland* 431 U.S. 494 (1977).

11. *Skinner v. Okla.* 316 U.S. 535 (1942).

12. *Griswold v. Conn.* 381 U.S. 479 (1965).

13. *Roe v. Wade* 410 U.S. 116 (1973).

14. The rules of general contractual capacity would exclude minors and other legal incompetents from binding themselves in reproductive agreements.

15. See, e.g., sec. 5 of the *Baby M* agreement, app. A to the New Jersey Supreme Court's decision, 14 *Fam. L. Rep.* (BNA) 2028; Brophy, A Surrogate Mother Contract to Bear a Child, 20 *J. Fam. L.* 263 (1981–82).

16. The most significant group of late abortion consumers today is composed of teenagers—inexperienced in sexual activity, ignorant of reproductive processes, uneducated in the use of contraception, unprepared for the responsibility of parenthood, and confused by contradictory cultural messages about sex and reproduction. Delayed abortion results from denial of the reality of pregnancy, fear of angry punitive parents, legal and administrative obstacles to abortion, and restricted Medicaid funding. See L. B. Francke, *The Ambivalence of Abortion* 179 (1978), and R. P. Petchesky, *Abortion and Woman's Choice: The State, Sexuality, and Reproductive Freedom* 148, 209, 347–48 (1984).

17. See, e.g., section 10 of the *Baby M* agreement, 14 *Fam. L. Rep.* (BNA) 2028; Brophy, at 277.

18. Section 13 of the *Baby M* agreement, 14 *Fam. L. Rep.* (BNA) 2029; cf. Brophy, at 280.

19. The most accepted test, amniocentesis, can be conducted at 16–20 weeks of gestation with analysis of the test culture taking 2–4 weeks. A new test—chorionic villi biopsy—can be performed as early as 8 weeks of gestation. Shell, A Head Start on Birth Defects, *Technology Rev.*, January 1984, 30. Also being researched is DNA technology. Fletcher, Emerging Ethical Issues in Fetal Therapy, in *Research Ethics* 293 (1983).

20. Compare Petchesky, at 347.

21. *Roe v. Wade* 410 U.S. 113 (1973).

22. 410 U.S. at 165–66.

23. Id., at 153, 214–15.

24. Compare B. Harrison, *Our Right to Choose: Toward a New Ethic of Abortion* 43, 46–47 (1983).

25. Compare Robertson, Procreative Liberty and the Control of Conception, Pregnancy, and Childbirth, 69 *Va. L. Rev.* 405, 429 (1983).

26. Again, I do not mean to imply any normative position as to the legal personality of the fetus. Its presence is significant in the scheme only as it affects the relations of the reproducing adults.

27. This might well be pertinent to the constitutional protection of the *father's* interest in abortion. In *Planned Parenthood of Mo. v. Danforth* 428 U.S. 52 (1976), the Supreme Court struck down a statute requiring spousal consent to abortion, reasoning that the wife's interests outweigh the husband's since she is more directly and immediately affected by the pregnancy. Under the analysis proposed here, the woman's general authority to decide on abortion indeed stems primarily from the norm that she bears the major child-rearing burden. I would suggest that unless the spouses had made express stipulation as to different allocation of the child-rearing responsibility, the woman should retain the authority. Even if stipulated otherwise, the woman could not be physically constrained to undergo or refrain from abortion, but usurpation of the husband's stipulated authority would be grounds for some kind of compensatory relief.

28. For further discussion of the father's standing in the abortion decision, see Shalev, A Man's Right to Be Equal: The Abortion Issue, 18 *Israel L. Rev.* (1983).

29. Fetal enzyme deficiencies or metabolic derangements can be alleviated by administering the missing substances to the pregnant woman. Rh incompatibility is treated through fetal blood transfusions. Actual surgery on the fetus to correct congenital anatomic defects that inhibit organ devel-

opment is still experimental. See Fletcher, Healing before Birth; An Ethical Dilemma, *Technology Rev.*, January 1984, 28; Note, Fetal Treatment, 307 *New Eng. J. Med.* 1651 (1982); Clewell, Fetal Surgery and Treatment, paper presented at the American Society of Law and Medicine Conference on Legal, Social, and Ethical Implications of New Reproductive and Prenatal Technologies, Cambridge, Mass., Oct. 29, 1984.

30. Fletcher (1983) at 307, and Fletcher (1984) at 34–35.

31. Legal coercion through a decree of specific performance or injunction is also highly impractical. In the British case of *Paton v. Trustee of BPAS* [1978] 2 All E.R. 987, the court refused to issue an injunction sought by a married man against his wife's contemplated abortion: "I ask the question," wrote the judge, " 'If an injunction were ordered what could be the remedy?' and I do not think I need to say any more than that no judge could ever consider sending a husband or wife to prison for breaking such an order." Compare *Jefferson v. Griffin Spalding Co. Hosp. Auth.* 247 Ga. 86, 274 S.E.2d 457 (1981), in which the Georgia Supreme Court upheld an order directing a woman to submit to cesarian-section birth on grounds of medical fetal indications. The woman not only removed herself from the hospital but also delivered a healthy baby without surgical intervention a few days later. Cf. Annas, Forced Cesarians: The Unkindest Cut of All, 12 *Hastings Center Rep.* 16 (1982).

32. Robertson, at 445–47.

33. See, e.g., Shaw, Conditional Prospective Rights of the Fetus, 5 *J. Legal Med.* 63 (1984); Simon, Parental Liability for Prenatal Injury, 14 *Colum. J. L. & Soc. Prob.* 47 (1978). Third-party liability for prenatal injury, specifically with regard to medical negligence, has become well established over the past twenty years and is a central factor in the current malpractice insurance crisis. The extension of liability to the mother also subjects her to medical control in an unprecedented way. For example, medical evidence suggests that consumption of moderate amounts of alcohol at about the time of conception and embryo implantation in the uterus results in a low-birthweight infant. The vagueness of this time period and the practical impossibility of identifying it at the time may lead to the far-reaching conclusion that a woman of childbearing age should be under a legal duty to abstain generally from consumption of alcohol.

34. See, e.g., Williams, Firing the Woman to Protect the Fetus: The Reconciliation of Fetal Protection with Employment Opportunity Goals under Title VII, 69 *Geo. L.J.* 41 (1981), for a gender-neutral policy that balances interests in fetal well-being with the employee's right to choose to

accept occupational hazards. Cf. Howard, Hazardous Substances in the Workplace: Implications for the Employment Rights of Women, 129 *U. Pa. L. Rev.* 98 (1981).

35. Ruddick and Wilcox, Operating on the Fetus, 12 *Hastings Center Rep.* 10, 13 (1982).

36. Atiyah, at 274–75.

37. See, e.g., Wexler, Rethinking the Modification of Child Custody Decrees, 94 *Yale L.J.* 757 (1985).

38. Compare Erickson, Contracts to Bear a Child, 65 *Cal. L. Rev.* 611, 621 (1978); Robertson, Surrogate Mothers: Not So Novel After All, 13 *Hastings Center Rep.* 28, 33 (1983).

39. Warnock Committee Report, secs. 8.11, 8.16.

40. On the central notion of the psychological parent, see J. Goldstein, A. Freud, and A. Solnit, *Beyond the Best Interests of the Child* 12–17 (1973).

41. Compare Robertson, 13 *Hastings Center Rep.*, at 30.

42. See Brophy.

Chapter 8: Woman as Economic Being

1. In January 1985 there were 108 IVF programs in the United States. Of these, 9 were run by women physicians and 4 by male-female teams. Lorber, Gender Politics and In Vitro Fertilization, paper presented at symposium, "Who Governs Reproduction?" Yale Law School, Nov. 2, 1985, 4 (ms. available from author).

2. S. Firestone, *The Dialectic of Sex* 188–89 (1970).

3. J. Mitchell, *Woman's Estate* 90, 105, 197–208 (1973). To do justice to Firestone, she did recognize that removal of the biological basis of women's oppression would not free them automatically and that the new technology, especially fertility control, could be used against them to reinforce the entrenched system of exploitation. Mitchell's critique appears to address Firestone's political program that required women to revolt and seize (temporary) control of the new technology as well as all the social institutions of childbearing and child rearing. Firestone, at 19.

4. A. Rich, *Of Woman Born* 24, 170 (1976).

5. Arditti, Klein, and Minden, *Introduction* to *Test-Tube Women* 2 (1984).

6. A. Dworkin, *Right-Wing Women* 174 (1983).

7. *Concise Oxford Dictionary,* 5th ed., 1964.

8. Dworkin, at 187.

9. Id., at 182.

10. *N.Y. Times,* July 31, 1987, p. B3.

11. G. Corea, *The Mother Machine* 170 (1985).

12. Lorber, at 1–3, 7–9.

13. Corea, at 222, 228; Dworkin, at 180–82.

14. Ince, Inside the Surrogate Industry, in *Test Tube Women,* at 99, 115.

15. The demographic profile of couples admitted to an in vitro fertilization program at Yale-New Haven Hospital was 95 percent white, almost half Catholic, highly educated, with two-career households, and in 15 percent of the women and 12 percent of the men biological children from previous relationships. Lorber, at 5.

16. Blakely, Surrogate Mothers: For Whom Are They Working?, *Ms.,* March 1983, 19–20; Corea, at 245.

17. A. Kessler-Harris, *Out to Work: A History of Wage-Earning Women in the United States* 180–81, 185–86 (1982).

18. *Lochner v. N.Y.* 198 U.S. 45 (1905).

19. *Muller v. Or.* 208 U.S. 402 (1908), 421.

20. Kessler-Harris, at 186–87, 190; Williams, Firing the Woman to Protect the Fetus: The Reconciliation of Fetal Protection with Employment Opportunity Goals under Title VII, 69 *Geo. L.J.* 641, 654–55 (1981).

21. Kessler-Harris, at 212; Law, Rethinking Sex and the Constitution, 132 *U. Pa. L. Rev.* 955, 957 (1984).

22. *Geduldig v. Aiello* 417 U.S. 484 (1974). For a critique of this ruling, see, e.g., Williams, The Equality Crisis: Some Reflections on Culture, Courts, and Feminism, 7 *Women's Rights L. Rptr* 175, 190–200 (1982); Siegel, Employment Equality under the Pregnancy Discrimination Act of 1978, 94 *Yale L.J.* 929 (1985).

23. MacKinnon, *Sexual Harassment of Working Women* 101 (1979).

24. Law, at 963–69; Scales, The Emergence of Feminist Jurisprudence: An Essay, 95 *Yale L.J.* 1373 (1986).

25. Law, at 965; Taub, Review: MacKinnon, Sexual Harassment of Working Women, 80 *Col. L. Rev.* 1686, 1695 (1980); Z. R. Eisenstein, *Feminism and Sexual Equality: Crisis in Liberal America* 241–43 (1984).

26. MacKinnon, Feminism, Marxism, Method and the State: Toward Feminist Jurisprudence, 8 *Signs* 635, 646 (1983).

27. MacKinnon, Pornography, Civil Rights, and Speech, 20 *Harv. Civ. Rts—Civ. Lib. L. Rev.* 1, 16–18 (1985). MacKinnon collaborated with

Dworkin—who objects to surrogacy as a new-wave prostitution—in creating the Minneapolis antipornography ordinance that defined pornography as a practice of sex discrimination, that is, one that subordinates women as a class on the basis of sex. Beyond providing legal redress for actual victims of pornography, the ordinance also made trafficking in pornography objectionable, which raises a debate in First Amendment terms. See *American Booksellers Ass'n v. Hudnut*, 771 F.2d 323 (1985)—ordinance held unconstitutional.

28. Antipornography activists seem to echo the conservative views of a major faction among nineteenth-century feminists who were active in the temperance movement. Echols, The New Feminism of Yin and Yang, in *Power of Desire: The Politics of Sexuality* 439, 446–47 (Snitow, Stansell, and Thompson, eds., 1983); Dimen, Politically Correct? Politically Incorrect? in *Pleasure and Danger: Exploring Female Sexuality* 138 (Vance, ed., 1984).

29. Echols, The Taming of the Id: Feminist Sexual Politics, 1968–83, in *Pleasure and Danger: Exploring Female Sexuality*, 50, 51–52. The problematic implications of stereotyping the human male as aggressive offender and the female as passive victim is illustrated by the crime of statutory rape, which enforces a double standard as regards intercourse between minors, making it criminal for the man but not for the woman. The underlying premise is that a minor woman cannot effectively consent to sexual intercourse because of the risk of pregnancy and must therefore be protected against herself by laws that punish the man. See *Michael M. v. Super. Ct.* 453 U.S. 57 (1981), upholding a California statutory rape statute in these terms. This reinforces the stereotype that women and not men are responsible for nurturing offspring and equates sexual freedom with reproductive irresponsibility. "The adolescent male sex drive, which, as both young women and men are taught, once triggered cannot take responsibility for itself or take no for an answer, becomes . . . the norm and rationale for adult male sexual behavior." Rich, Compulsory Heterosexuality and Lesbian Existence, in *The Signs Reader: Women, Gender, and Scholarship* 139, 153 (1983). Cf. Williams (1982), at 185–86; Law, at 998–1001. An analogous stereotype, much overlooked by feminist analysis, is that of man as aggressor in war. In *Rotsker v. Goldberg* 450 U.S. 455 (1981), the U.S. Supreme Court upheld a draft registration law applicable to men only, reasoning that the purpose of the draft was to provide combat troups and that differential treatment was justified since women were excluded from combat. As Williams points out, our notions of gender equality appear to reach their cultural limits when we address the male sex-role of combat warrior. Williams (1982), 181–85.

30. Vance, Pleasure and Danger: Towards a Politics of Sexuality, in *Pleasure and Danger: Exploring Female Sexuality*, 1, 6–7.

31. Id., 24.

32. See Gordon, Why Nineteenth-Century Feminists Did Not Support 'Birth Control' and Twentieth-Century Feminists Do: Feminism, Reproduction, and the Family, in *Rethinking the Family* 40, 51 (Thorne and Freeman, eds., 1978).

33. D. Dinnerstein, *The Mermaid and the Minotaur: Sexual Arrangements and Human Malaise* (1976); N. Chodorow, *The Reproduction of Mothering: Psychoanalysis and the Sociology of Gender* (1978).

34. Compare Landes and Posner, The Economics of the Baby Shortage, 7 *J. Legal Studies* 323, 336–37 (1978).

35. Id., at 338.

36. Wisotsky, Exposing the War on Cocaine: The Futility and Destructiveness of Prohibition, 1983 *Wis. L. Rev.* 1305, 1424–25.

37. Pritchard, A Market for Babies, 34 *U. Toronto L. Rev.* 341, 347 (1984).

38. Id., at 351; Landes and Posner, at 344–45.

39. Pritchard, at 357.

40. Id., at 353.

41. Eisenstein, at 16; Olsen, The Family and the Market: A Study of Ideology and Legal Reform, 96 *Harv. L. Rev.* 1497 (1983). Olsen points out, at 1501–04, that there are analogies between the classic laissez-faire argument against regulation of the free market and the argument against state interference with the private family. Both posit that the market and the family exist independently of the state and are characterized by intrinsic "natural" forces that resist and nullify any but the most radical measures to impose state control.

42. Chodorow, at 9; M. O'Brien, *The Politics of Reproduction* 93, 116ff. (1981).

43. E. Zaretsky, *Capitalism, the Family, and Personal Life* 26–31 (1976).

44. Olsen, at 1520–22.

45. Dworkin, at 202–03.

46. Olsen, at 1510–11, 1521–23.

47. MacKinnon, 8 *Signs* (1983), at 675; cf. C. MacKinnon, *Feminism Unmodified: Discourses on Life and Law* 93–102 (1987).

48. See. e.g., Remick, *Preface* to *Comparable Worth and Wage Discrimination: Technical Possibilities and Political Realities* ix–xi (Remick, ed., 1984); Steinberg, A Want of Harmony, in id., 16–19.

49. Steinberg, at 17–23. These patterns are often justified as merely re-

flecting marketplace forces beyond the control of the individual employer. For example, in *AFSCME v. Wash.* 578 F. Supp. 846 (1983), the U.S. District Court found a 20 percent disparity in salary between predominantly male and female jobs on a comparable worth analysis. It concluded that the state had "historically engaged in employment discrimination on the basis of sex" and ordered injunctive relief and award of back pay. The decision was, however, reversed on appeal, on the ground that the disparity was created by market forces rather than the state. 770 F.2d 1401 (1985).

50. Frug, Securing Job Equality for Women: Labor Market Hostility to Working Mothers, 59 *Boston U. L. Rev.* 55, 55–59 (1979); cf. Eisenstein, 115.

51. M. Janssen-Jurreit, *Sexism: The Male Monopoly on History and Thought* 351 (1982).

52. Although Western culture proclaims the moral value of human life over and above any other value, a degree of hypocrisy rests in that attitude. Thus, the male sex role of warrior conditions young men to prepare themselves to sacrifice their lives in their nation's political interest. While opponents of legal abortion characterize it as infanticide, Oriana Fallaci points out that there is "no form of infanticide worse than war: war is mass infanticide postponed to the age of twenty." Fallaci, *Letter to a Child Never Born* 77 (1982).

53. O'Brien, at 60.

54. Janssen-Jurreit, at 351.

55. O'Brien, at 158–59.

56. See, e.g., P. Singer and D. Wells, *The Reproductive Revolution* 107–08 (1984); Waller, Borne for Another, 10 *Monash L. Rev.* 113, 126 (1984); Krimmel, The Case against Surrogate Parenting, 13 *Hastings Center Rep.* 35, 36 (1983).

57. The biblical texts unequivocally describe Hagar, Bilhah, and Zilpah as slaves of their respective barren matrons, using the terms *shifchah* and *amah* (Gen. 16:1, 30:3, 9). These are to be strictly distinguished from the concubine (*pilegesh*), who was one of a harem of freeborn or freed women belonging directly to the patriarch as secondary wives. See L. Epstein, *Marriage Laws in the Bible and Talmud* 34–62 (1942).

58. O'Brien, at 60.

59. Mitchell, at 106–07.

60. S. de Beauvoir, *The Second Sex* xv (1949; reprint 1968).